Miley Cyrus

MILES TO GO

MILES TO GO

by **MILEY CYRUS**

with Hilary Liftin

DISNEY ✳ HYPERION BOOKS

New York

Dedicated to my first love! The only man who understands me. The one who will forever own the key to my heart. The one I am lucky enough to call not only my best friend but my hero. This book is in memory of my Pappy. I will always love you! Thank you for answering my prayers........
xo Miley
P.S. I Miss You!

BEFORE THE BEFORE

It's weird to be doing an introduction to an introduction. But since this is the first time my book will be in paperback, it seems as good a time as any to do a little refreshing.

The other day I heard someone say, "Youth is wasted on the young." I don't remember who said it, or if they were older or younger or in the middle, but the line hit me and made me think. Sort of like when you see a truly beautiful sunset and it just settles in the back of your mind, makes you wonder about all the sunsets you've seen before. I don't want my youth to be wasted. The miles are zooming by and I know that if I don't slow down, I'll miss some of the best ones. That is part of what I loved so much about working on this book. Like I said, *Miles to Go* is one of those stopping points. Where I get to step back, take a breath, and count my blessings.

And yes, I have so much to be thankful for.

I am in love with sunsets right now!

7 things I've done since this book came out

1. made a new CD
2. made a new movie
3. hung out with friends and family
4. recorded a song with an old friend
5. saw Hannah Montana get to the big screen!
6. got a goat! (Thanks Daddy!)
7. became addicted to Twitter! (and then deleted it!)

I told you I'm way into sunsets right now, and that is mostly because of Tybee Island, Georgia. It's where we filmed *The Last Song*. The movie is based on a Nicholas Sparks* book and Veronica "Ronnie" Miller, the character I play, could not be any more different from Hannah Montana. I loved the challenge.

*Love his work!

2

The movie is magic. But so is Tybee Island. I'm pretty sure the island actually has some kind of magic calming ability. From the moment I got there, I was so happy. I'd sit on the deck of the house we rented with my mom and drink tea and just look out at the water. I loved playing guitar out on that deck, watching the dolphins and just getting back to *me*. I hated to leave. When I did, I cried for days straight.*

*I'll get to that later!

My mom kept telling me that I was lucky, because I had had the chance to experience something so magical and amazing that would live on in the movie and in the friendships I made.** It took a while, but

**Love you, cast and crew!

then I came around, and now I know what she said is true.

I wouldn't have figured that all out, though, if I hadn't stopped to let the emotions soak in. I'm trying hard to keep these memories close to my heart. I want to be able to pull them out on a rainy day, just like I can pull this book out years from now and remember. Like I said, I don't want my youth wasted and I don't want it forgotten.

Of course, there are some things I would LIKE to forget. Who doesn't have a moment they would like to erase? I don't mean to complain and I'm not trying to play the sympathy card—but when you are in the spotlight, people like to make sure you never forget the bad moments. There are a lot of haters out there. Dad always tells me I need to grow thick skin and not care what people say, but it's pretty hard. I like to say what's on my mind. I like to do what I want to do. It's all part of being a kid, and my parents and friends want me to be a kid as much as I can. But sometimes people like to say hurtful things. Tell me I'm pretending to be deep. And I guess maybe I am growing a thicker skin, because I'm starting to realize that I can't please everyone. I'm lucky I have the opportunities I have. I thank God every day for them.

Now I have another one of those markers to plant. **This is at a new point in my life, and things are totally changing. But like the sunsets I saw on Tybee Island, the miles I've already gone are going to stay with me.**

You know you do!

INTRODUCTION

Okay, this is gonna sound like a weird place to start, but I think a lot about my hands. I was born left-handed. My dad is also a lefty, but he's absolutely convinced that I'm right-handed. I think it's because he has always said lefties have to "learn the world backwards," and I know he has had a hard time finding a left-handed guitar every now and then. . . . Whatever the reason, from the time I started to write, he had me use my right hand. It worked. In the rest of my life I'm left-handed, but I do write with my right hand. So if you don't like my handwriting—talk to my dad.

Just to mess with my left-handed self a little more, I came across a book about calligraphy and started teaching myself to write Chinese characters. With my right hand. On a plane. I was flying a chartered jet from Los Angeles to New York. The flight was turbulent, the ink spilled at least twice, and I managed to get it all over myself, the paper, the seats of the plane, and, when I tried to clean up the mess, the bathroom. My mom was yelling at me for getting ink everywhere, but I was really into it.

The word *calligraphy* is Greek for "beautiful writing." Believe me, people, if the Greeks saw what I was doing they'd make up a new word for it. But I was immediately obsessed. I drew the characters for "love," "luck," "life," and "knowledge" over and over again, first slowly and carefully like a kindergartner learning to write, then faster and better.

one of my first tries.

It's a good thing the plane wasn't equipped for skywriting, or I probably would have tried to convince the pilot to take a stab at the sign for "Rock on." There's got to be an ancient Chinese character for that, right?

7 hobbies I obsessed over for 5 seconds

1. calligraphy
2. beading
3. knitting (for two seconds)
4. scrapbooking
5. reading the life story of Einstein
6. being a marine biologist
7. high fashion

Some people believe that your handwriting tells all your secrets—that the slants and loops and dots of a scribbled to-do list or a note passed in class reveal all there is to know about a person. It's a cool idea, but really I think the only thing anyone can tell about me from my handwriting is that I'm supposed to be writing with my other hand. I do almost everything else—brush my hair, open doors, hold a fork, and carry the reins of my horses—with my left hand. And, you know, my Dad had a point—**I do think the world feels a little bit backward sometimes even when I'm trying to keep everything going in the right direction.**

Maybe because I've felt so aware of them, I've always been superprotective of my hands. I know, I know: weird.* But I just feel as though my hands are important. My energy comes from them. Everything I do comes from them.

* You might be reading this word a lot in this book. Or at least thinking it.

My right hand is for art. I use it to play guitar and to write. My left hand is for caring. For combing my little sister's hair. For holding hands with friends. For comforting Sofie, my puppy, as we fall asleep. (And occasionally for slapping my brother Braison upside the head when he's picking on me. I know—but everybody has their limits!)

I let both my hands wander freely on a piano, searching for the right notes. My hands steer my thoughts when I write in my journal. They riffle through my Bible, finding truths. The beat for a new song emerges as I drum on a tabletop. I feel my way through hard times. I want all I do to be artistic and loving. Who I am and what I say and whatever hope and joy I may spread—it all comes from my own two hands.

Am I right-handed? Am I left-handed? Am I neither? Am I a singer, or an actor? Am I a public person, or am I a private person? Why can't I be all these things? I'm on TV. I'm writing a book. But I also love staying at home with my family. And I feel alone—in a good way—inside my head. Am I the person you know from television, photographs, even this book? Or are we all, each of us, more elusive, and harder to define? Who am I to say?

Most people know me as Hannah Montana, but Hannah is a television character. She's fiction. Sure, I've put a lot of myself into her. I've tried to make her come to life. But that doesn't make her real, and it doesn't make her *me*. This is my very own book—my first chance to tell my own story in my own words. But to tell my story, I have to talk about Hannah. And that's okay. Because I think that's why people relate to both Hannah Montana and Miley Stewart—my alter egos on TV. **There are multiple sides to all of us. Who we are—and who we might be if we follow our dreams.**

It seems like I'm always answering questions about myself: I do interviews on TV, radio, and for magazines; I talk to paparazzi and strangers on the street. Over and over I tell people (and so far it's always true) that the tour's going so great, the show is so much fun, and I'm so proud of my album. But nobody ever comes up to me and asks, "Hey, how do you feel about your hands? How are they connected to your art? What do they mean to you?" This book is the place where I can explain and joke and muse and explore what's truly important to me. I want to answer the questions I'm never asked. I want to let my guard down. I want to talk about what music means to me, and I want to show that my life isn't all sunshine and

Surpr
surpr

rainbows. It's not like I've never been hurt or broken. I've felt pressured, unwanted, sad, bored, and lonely. And I've felt great joy and gratitude. I want to share who I really am—not the straight-edged, Photoshopped, glossy girl who appears on magazine covers, but a Nashville-born middle child who loves Marilyn Monroe and hates vegetables and has always had some rather funny ideas about her own hands.

When I started working on this book I was fifteen, and I turned sixteen by the time I finished it. I'm pretty young to be writing about my life. But I'm considered pretty young for plenty of the things I do and enjoy. There's nothing wrong with being young. Young people have lots of energy! We have lots to say. I've never had a shortage of thoughts, ideas, or opinions. I know I'm still near the beginning of my life. I'm having an incredible journey, and it's going superfast. So I want to plant a mile marker right here—at this particular bend in the road—before its image starts to fade as I keep moving forward. I hope you can kick back and ~~enjoy the ride~~* hang out with me for a while.

* Forget the cheesy driving metaphor.

See!
I improved.

MILE ONE

Think Outside the Bowl

Lyric and Melody

For a while I had two fish. I was obsessed with them. Their names were Lyric and Melody. Sometimes, when I should have been writing, I'd sit and watch them swimming in circles in their bowl. Outside, in the pastures, our horses ran free; but I would stare at those two fish swimming in their glass world forever. They were so beautiful. I could just put my two hands around that bowl and know that there was something wonderful in there. Life in a jar.

Life in a jar is a miracle, but it's also a trap. Lyric and Melody were stuck, destined to thread the same line through the water over and over again. Their worlds never expanded. They could never have Nemo adventures, never find out who they were. I'd gaze into their small world, looking for a song. *Think outside the bowl.* That's what I told myself. *Think outside the bowl.* **I didn't want to be stuck like the fish, stuck seeing only the world that was right in front of me, stuck swimming in circles.** But when I was eleven, in sixth grade, it was hard to imagine any world beyond the one where I was stuck.

I wasn't *always* stuck. And I did get unstuck. Every story has a beginning, a middle, and an end, and so does this one. But I'm only sixteen—let's face it, this is all "the beginning"—so to start with the day I was born and tell you every major milestone (I lost a tooth! I turned ten! I got a new bike!) until my sweet sixteen isn't how I want to do this.

Instead, I want to start with sixth grade. It was the last year that I'd be known as just Miley Cyrus. It was a dividing point—what I now think of as my life before and my life after.

Not All Butterflies
and Flowers

To say sixth grade was not a good year would be the understatement of the decade. When I found out that pilot season—when all the auditions for TV shows happen in Los Angeles—overlapped with the beginning of school that September, I spent a good hour on the floor of my room bawling. That meant if I wanted even a shot at being on TV, I'd have to start school in Nashville a couple of weeks late. At the time, the idea of missing any school seemed awful.

We'd just come back from a year in Canada, near Toronto, where my dad was starring in the TV series *Doc*. He and my mom had been commuting back and forth for a few years, but the summer before I went

If only I had known

into fifth grade we all missed him so much that my mom moved us up there.

She homeschooled me that year, so now I was coming back to my old school after a year's absence. ~ Scary!

Not only that, I knew perfectly well that the first few weeks of school are when everything gets sorted out—you meet your teachers, you find your friends, you figure out if the new school clothes you bought are acceptable—or completely *un*acceptable. **The cool people find each other. The smart people find each other. Me and all the other in-between artsy people realize we'd better join forces and make the best of it.** If you miss all that fun, you risk being an outcast. A loser. If you've been through middle school, then you know what I'm talking about. If you haven't yet, well then . . . hang in there. It gets better, I promise. Either way, you can imagine, missing school was far from ideal. But if I wanted to be a performer—and I did—then there really wasn't a choice. I had to go to Los Angeles.

I didn't want to be the weird wannabe actress.

I wasn't exactly expecting to just show up back at school and be one of the cool girls. The farm in

Tennessee where we lived when we weren't in Toronto was kind of isolated, so there weren't any neighborhood kids for me to practice being friends with. I grew up playing with my brothers and sisters, but I was just as comfortable hanging out with my parents and their friends.

It didn't help that I always had too much energy. There was no way I could sit still and focus for hours on end. People didn't know exactly how to handle me. It's not that I was trying to be disrespectful, but I. Could. Not. Be quiet. On my first day of school one year, my teacher told me I'd get detention if I said one more word. I turned to my friend and whispered, "One more word." Boom! Detention. For whispering. On the first day of school. I'm lucky the teacher didn't hear exactly what I said, or who knows what would have happened to me.

At school I always wanted to be my own person and wasn't shy about it. I had a lot to say. I stood out in drama and music. I made good grades. I had huge dreams. Not exactly the formula for "cool." Most kids worry about not fitting in; I worried about not standing out. I wanted to feel unique, quirky, different. But standing out by missing the crucial beginning of school wasn't exactly what I had in mind.

Anyway, when I got back to Nashville for sixth grade—two weeks after school had started—my old friends seemed happy to see me, and life felt back to normal. I started to think I'd dodged a bullet and that I had worried for nothing. But slowly I realized that wasn't the case. One of my closer friends, let's call her Rachel,* and I started drifting toward a group of girls in our class. They weren't the "cool" girls or the "mean" girls. I didn't really know what their deal was then, and I can't stereotype them now. But for some reason, they were the group I wanted to fit in with.

*Obviously, not her real name.

The first sign of trouble was the teeniest, tiniest thing you could possibly imagine. We were standing near our lockers after math. I made a joke, and the leader—she'll be MG, for Mean Girl—rolled her eyes. That was it: a tiny gesture—it went by in a second. But this was sixth grade. *Everything* means *something* in sixth grade. What did I do in response? Nothing, of course. I mean, if you've been through sixth grade, you know how it goes. If I had said something straightforward like "What's up with the nasty eye-roll?" MG would have just said something patronizing like "I have no idea what you're talking about," and I'd be humiliated. A feeling I loathe more than anything. So I acted like I hadn't seen it. I put it out of my head.

But the signs kept coming. A few days later, I put my tray down at lunch and thought I heard a snarl. *A snarl?* The next week, I came in wearing a new jean jacket. I said, "I love my outfit today." One of them sneered, "You do?" and gave me a look that shriveled me up into a puny dried pea on the floor. From yesterday's dinner.

Now I knew I wasn't just being paranoid. I was an outcast. Why were my "friends" turning on me? I had no idea. But there you have it. **Welcome to sixth-grade social hell.**

yes, that was the thing in sixth grade.

On the Other Hand . . .

You know how it feels on a hot summer day to dive into the crisp relief of a cold swimming pool? Well, that's how it felt when I came home from school after a particularly hard day to be told that Disney had called. Margot, a talent agent who'd taken an interest in me, let us know that Disney had asked her to send tapes of all the girls she represented between the ages of eleven and sixteen. They wanted a tape of me reading for the part of Lilly, the best friend of a girl named Chloe Stewart in a new TV show called *Hannah Montana*.

From the very first time my parents and I read the script, we knew that Chloe Stewart was my dream part. Chloe's alter ego, Hannah Montana, was a rock star. The actress who played both parts would be singing Hannah Montana's songs. Singing *and* acting. Both were dreams of mine, and if I landed this role, I wouldn't have to put either one aside. After my dad read the part, he just kept saying, "That's made for Miley. Miley's made for that."

But, heck, I'd be happy to play Lilly. Or lucky to be Chloe Stewart's talking houseplant, for that matter. So we made a tape, sent it in, and almost immediately got a call from Disney asking me to make another audition tape—and this time they wanted me to read the part of Hannah. I was so psyched. Seriously, my shrieks probably scared the poor horses out in the fields. In my head, I was already dropping everything to move to L.A. Sure, Hannah was supposed to be fifteen, and I was twelve. Twelve-ish. Okay, I was eleven. That was a problem. But still—they knew how old I was and they'd asked for the tape anyway, so it must not matter.

Except it did. We sent the second tape in, and the very next day we got an e-mail saying that I was too young and too small for Hannah. I was bummed.

Hello? Didn't they know that from the Lilly tape?

22

No—what's ten *times* bummed? That was me. My dad said, "Disney just made a big mistake. My intuition tells me that you are Hannah Montana."

All I could think was, *So much for Dad's intuition.* Now let's return to our regularly scheduled torture: sixth grade.

Operation MMM

Is there a guide for how to torture eleven-year-old girls? If not, those girls I'd started hanging with—you remember, my "friends"—could write one.* In the winter of that year, every day brought a creative new tactic in Operation Make Miley Miserable. They sent me mean notes. They stole my books and made me late to class. They made fun of my clothes and my hair. They told Rachel—the friend who had become tight with them at the same time as I did—that if she sat with me at lunch they'd have it in for her too. So I sat at a table by myself day after day, looking at the goth kids, wondering what I'd look like with black hair and chains. I've since decided: not so good.

The list goes on: Rachel stopped speaking to me.

* What am I saying? That's a terrible idea.

When I wanted to try out for the school cheerleading team, my so-called friends told the principal that I'd cheated and learned the tryout dances in advance. Total lie, but the principal believed them, and I wasn't allowed to try out for the squad. Oh, and I'll never forget how one of them was nice to me for a few days. She said she wanted the "fight" to be over. She got me to tell her exactly what I thought about "our friends"— that I didn't understand why they didn't like me, that I felt like they were being mean—then she went back to them and told them I was a snob. She'd been faking it. Looking back I think maybe she was the one who should have been an actress.

At least I still had my competitive cheerleading squad outside of school.

Me = total sucker.

If this sounds like run-of-the-mill Judy Blume *Tales of a* Sixth-*Grade Nothing*, well, it was. I wasn't oblivious to issues like world hunger or pandemics. I knew my problems were relatively puny. But they were mine. And they felt heavier than the world on my shoulders. So, if you want to know if I liked school back then, the answer was definitely no.

The First Dream

Luckily, I had a whole other world outside of school. The acting thing was only a small part of my life then. I had started doing competitive cheerleading when I was six, and for a long time it really was my everything.

My mom got me into it. We lived on a big farm, which was incredible, but there were no neighbors nearby, no kids around for us to play with besides each other. Which wasn't bad, in my mind. I loved the animals, and I loved hanging out with my cool big brother, Trace (I call him Trazz), my amazing big sister, Brandi, my little brother, Braison (I call him Brazz), and my baby sister, Noah—when she came along. But my mom wanted me to have some friends besides horses, chickens, and my brothers and sisters. Not in that order. (Okay, maybe in that order.) Since Mom had loved cheerleading as a kid, she wanted me to give it a try.

Just Kidding, guys!

The first day I was supposed to go to practice, I was not happy. I begged: *Please* don't make me go! What's wrong with having horses and chickens and little brothers as my only friends? They won't let me down, they won't laugh at me—sure, they smell a little (sorry, Brazz)—but that's okay. I'm not shallow.

Maybe my mom was right about the whole farm-makes-you-shy thing.

It may not be obvious from my life today, but being around new people makes me anxious. Just the idea of walking into a room of strangers keeps me up at night. Anyway, I knew that my dad was on my side about the whole not going to cheerleading thing. He traveled so much that he just wanted us kids around whenever he was home. But my mom stuck to her guns, and I went. And because moms are right way too much of the time, I loved it instantly.*

* Don't tell my mom I said that!

Cheerleading took a lot of time. A lot. I was at the gym every day. We worked out. We tumbled. We practiced two-and-a-half-minute routines over and over and over again. I became best friends with Lesley and the other girls on the team, and my mom became friends with their moms. We traveled together to competitions, stayed in motels, swam, goofed around, did our hair and makeup with our moms, and had intense, incredibly hard-core competitions. I was really into it.

♡ cheerleading 4ever

Sometimes I was *too* into it. One time I got really sick right before a competition in Gatlinburg, Tennessee. I could not stop throwing up. You know, one of those stomach things where even if you take a sip of water, you retch? Yeah, it was bad. But how long could it last? I was sure I'd be better in time for the competition. So I made my mom take me, and I spent the whole four-and-a-half-hour drive lying down in the backseat with a garbage can next to me, sleeping, throwing up, and sleeping some more. We got to the hotel in Gatlinburg and I was no better, but I still wanted to compete. My coach said there was no way I could do it. She tried to stop me, but I insisted. I knew I could do it if I pushed myself.

Thirty minutes before we were supposed to go on, I pulled myself out of bed, showered, and we drove to the meet. I went out, did the routine, walked off the stage, and threw up into a trash can. But I did it. And that was what mattered to me.

When we would get in the car after every competition, even if we lost, my mom would say, "Here's your trophy!" and hand me a gleaming trophy with my name on it. Growing up, my room was full of trophies. All from my mom, the biggest and best fan a girl could have.* I may not have deserved every single one of those trophies, but the Gatlinburg trophy—that one I *know* I earned.

* I ♥ you Mom!

A Long Pit Stop

Cheerleading was my safe haven, the one place where I knew I had friends I could trust to the ends of the earth. Or at least to catch me when I was flying through the air, which was a little more likely than reaching the ends of the earth, anyway. But at school I had no such safety net. And things were getting worse.

I still have no idea how the Anti-Miley Club got a janitor's key to the school bathroom, but one day I was on my way to science class, and they shoved me in and locked it. I was trapped. I banged on the door until my fists hurt. Nobody came. I tried to open the window, but it was stuck.* It dawned on me that everyone was already in class. Nobody would come

* Note to self: in case of fire do not attempt to exit via bathroom window.

to use the bathroom for at least forty minutes. I sat down on the floor and waited. **I spent what felt like an hour in there, waiting for someone to rescue me, wondering how my life had gotten so messed up.**

I looked at the line of stalls, the row of mirrors, the unyielding windows, and thought about my two fish, swimming around and around in their bowl. How had I gotten here? Had I asked for it? Did I deserve it? Would it ever end? I knew the capitals of all fifty states. I could do a back handspring on the sidewalk. But I had no clue as to why this was happening. I was friendless, lonely, and miserable. The only bright spot was that if I had to use the bathroom, at least I was in the right place!

When Disney Calls

It was as if someone wanted to make it up to me for what was going on at school. Not long after the bathroom incident, I got another surprise call—this time it was Disney saying they wanted me to come to L.A. to audition in person for *Hannah Montana*. It was the middle of the school year! Score! I could miss school—i.e., Torture 101. But then I remembered. I also had major cheerleading commitments.

Missing just a single practice was a big deal. The choreography relies on everyone showing up. After all, you can't have a pyramid without the top girl. Actually, it's even worse to try making a pyramid without one of the bottom girls!

Somehow my mom got me excused from practice.

Don't try this at home!

I flew to L.A., anxiously ran lines with Mom, hurried to get to the audition on time, could barely contain my excitement, opened the door to the waiting room, and—there were fifty other would-be Hannahs waiting to be seen. My mom and I looked at each other. We had thought I was a finalist. I guess we thought wrong. We joked that they had enough Hannahs there to name one after every state, not just Montana. (Hannah Indiana, Hannah Connecticut, Hannah Idaho . . .) I know, I know—but we had a *lot* of time to kill in that waiting room.

7 places I want to go

1. Fiji
2. Australia
3. Italy
4. Hawaii
5. Germany
6. Spain
7. North Carolina

The waiting room for the *Hannah Montana* auditions was like the waiting room in a busy doctor's office. There were old magazines, odd smells, tons of tension—and we were all about to be examined. Some of the moms who were waiting with their daughters had way too much perfume on, giving me an insta-headache. The only saving grace was that at least we wouldn't have to get any vaccinations. Although I was pretty certain that not getting the part would hurt at least as much and the pain would last longer.

As we waited, and waited, and waited some more, I could see that some of the girls and their moms were sizing us up. My mom, thank goodness, has never been "that" mom. She ignored the looks, but I couldn't. It was tense in that room. You couldn't help thinking about who was prettiest or best prepared or most talented. As I sat there, I snuck peeks at the other girls. I didn't recognize any of them—not that I expected to. I had done some auditioning, but I hadn't exactly been going all over town.

Most of the girls were older than I was and much taller. Many of them were beautiful. Some had shiny black hair. Others had long blond hair. Some had glowing white teeth. I looked at how they were dressed, how they did their makeup, and how they wore their hair. On looks alone, I was pretty sure most of those girls could land the role hands down. And I could only imagine what kind of experience they had had. I felt way out of my league. Auditions were by far the most scary, nerve-racking moments I ever had. Each one was like taking a test. I liked to perform, so I was always excited, but I also always really wanted the job, so the anxiety was huge. But on that particular day, the cheerleader in me woke up.

My cheerleading coach, Chastity, was really tough. In Nashville, some people treated me differently because I was the singer Billy Ray Cyrus's daughter. They'd cut me slack because my dad was *somebody*. Not Chastity. If I messed up, she made me run laps just like everyone else. If anything, she was tougher on me. I was afraid to fly—to be the person at the top of the stunt who soars through the air—but she had me work one-on-one with the stunt trainer. I wasn't the best tumbler, but she made me practice until my back handspring was just right. I bounced off my head until I felt like I'd been spinning in circles for hours.

Chastity didn't care how long it took me. She was proud, so long as I didn't quit. She always said, *"Can't is not a word."* Chastity taught me that when I wanted something, I had to work hard for it. I wanted this part badly. Who was to say that these polished L.A. girls were any better than I was? When they finally called my name, I was ready.

In the audition room, I faced a panel of ten people. I stood there, dressed in my short little skirt and T-shirt—Abercrombie'd out. You want them to remember you, so I made sure to be outgoing. Um, it wasn't exactly a stretch. For once in my life, it was good that I talked too much. I just had to make sure to be myself instead of letting my nerves take over. The casting people asked me to read from a script, then to sing. I sang a little bit from *Mamma Mia!* As at most auditions, they gave me comments, like "Can you try it a little brighter?" or "Read it again as if you're really annoyed at your brother." (It's funny, I was so nervous and had no idea then who those people on the panel were. They were just intimidating strangers. Now they're the people I work closely with every day.)

When I came out of the room I had no idea how I'd

done. And I couldn't relax yet even though it was over. Sort of. The most stressful part of the whole auditioning ordeal is that you can't go home until they tell you you're done. You have to hang out in the waiting room, watching other girls get called back in, wondering if you're going to be called in to read something different or to sing again. And you never know why you're being called back in. Or not being called back in but still made to stay. Do they like you? Do they love you? Does one person hate you? Are they worried about your hair? Your height? They never give you the tiniest hint of hope.

I did my best, but we ended up going home to Nashville with no good news. And then, a couple weeks later, I got another call. "You're a finalist!" Okay, this was the real thing. Maybe I had my ticket out of sixth grade after all. Again I begged out of cheerleading. Two strikes. One more and Chastity would kick me off the team. I flew to L.A., anxiously ran lines with Mom, hurried to get to the audition on time, could barely contain my excitement, opened the door to the waiting room, and—there were thirty other would-be Hannahs waiting to be seen. Sound familiar?

I was starting to feel like one of those balls that's attached to a paddle by a rubber band. Each time I got smacked away, they pulled me back just so they could smack me again. Well, it was a little gentler than that. But I was eleven. It was a roller coaster.* In the faces of those thirty girls I saw the grim reality. I had barely made any progress. I was definitely going back to sixth grade.

* Is that a more friendly metaphor?

Make Your Own Dreams

I couldn't escape school but I *could* focus on other things. We had a huge cheerleading competition coming up, so I threw myself into training and tried to forget about bullies and auditions. My life only sucked from eight a.m. to three p.m. Then I went to the gym and pushed it all out of my head.

And then, when I had just about really and truly given up hope, we got another call from Margot the talent agent. Disney wanted to see me *again*. What were they doing, cutting one girl at a time *American Idol*-style? This time there was no shrieking and disrupting of the animals' peaceful farm life. Instead of feeling excited, I just felt tired of it all. I told my mom I didn't want to go back. I figured it was going to be the same thing all over again. I was completely focused on cheerleading. My team wanted me. My team *needed* me. My team didn't make me fly cross-country over and over again only to send me home with nothing. My mom was over it too. She said it stressed her out. But then Margot told us that Judy Taylor, the head of casting, had said, "You can't pass on this. They're really serious about Miley. They've seen so many girls, and they keep coming back to her."

Missing this competition would mean dropping off the team. **I had to choose between cheerleading and auditioning.** To this day it's the hardest decision I've ever had to make. My mom said it was up to me, but she wanted me to have perspective, to make an informed decision. She said, "Honey, are you *sure*? I think you're amazing, but the chances of getting this role are still slim to none. You have no experience. We already know they think you're too small and too young. You have the rest of your life to do this. If you go, you may end up sacrificing cheerleading for nothing."

My dad's advice was simpler: "You have to go. This part is meant for you." (He really has a lot of faith in that intuition of his.) They told me to take my time and think about it really seriously.

7 things that help me fall asleep

1. a Fine Frenzy CD
2. reading the life story of Einstein
3. counting
4. thinking about my family
5. responding to e-mails
6. business meetings
7. snuggling up 2 my doggie, Sofie

So I thought long and hard. Cheerleading wasn't just my passion. It was my salvation that year. It was the only way I was surviving sixth grade. If I quit and then didn't get the part, which we all knew was the most likely sequence of events, I'd be left with nothing. But I didn't plan to be a cheerleader for the rest of my life. This was my chance. And I was scared out of my mind.

I have always believed that the greatest opportunities in life come with fear and risk. I realized that taking the risk was like soaring in a cheerleading stunt and having faith that someone would catch me. Maybe cheerleading had been training me for this moment. **I knew it was too much to hope for, but Hannah Montana was my dream role, and it was closer than ever. I wasn't about to give up now.** It was back to L.A.

The dreams that you hold for your future are what you dream about at night. They're always at the back of your mind. They're what your heart desires. They keep you going. Accept reality and have a backup plan, but always follow your dreams no matter what.

✳   ✳   ✳

This time there were only *two* other girls in the
waiting room. One of them was Taylor Momsen, who
had been in *Spy Kids 2* and now stars in *Gossip Girl*.
She was gorgeous, with long, blond hair. The other
one was sixteen years old. I was like a foot shorter
than both of them. When I got called into the audition
room, I read scenes for the executives over and over
again. I sang songs for them. I talked to them so they
could "get to know me." I read more scenes. I sang
more songs. I read songs. I sang scenes. I would have
hung wallpaper while wearing a tutu if I thought it
would prove I was meant to play Hannah.

It was a long day, and *finally* it was over. My mom,
my maternal grandmother (Mammie), and I were
staying at the Universal Studios theme park so we'd
have something fun to do if the trip turned out to be a
bust. Auditions done, we went to dinner at a restaurant
there called Daily Grill. We sat down, got our drinks,
and I promptly spilled Mammie's entire Dr Pepper
all over my white skirt.

As I was yanking paper napkins out of the
dispenser as fast as I could, Margot called. She and

Things did not look good for me.

See? Life imitates sitcoms imitating life.

43

my mother talked a little bit, then my mom hung up and turned to me. "They want us to go back to the studio *right now*," she told me. "They want to test you with another girl they have for Lilly. Margot said we should drop everything." I looked at my Dr Pepper–soaked skirt and said, "I thought I already did." I couldn't go like that! But they were sending a car for us! We sprinted back to the hotel so I could change before the car came.

My heart racing and palms sweating,* I tested with the Lilly actress, a sweet girl with very dark hair. She and I whispered excitedly. We were the ones! Weren't we? It seemed so promising. At the end I thought they were going to tell me I had the part. Instead, they just said thank you and sent me back to Nashville.

* I know. Real Professional.

At first I made my mom call the agent every day to see if there was any news, but there was never any news. Weeks went by. Finally, we just stopped calling.

The Cafeteria

I never told anyone at school that I was auditioning in L.A., but it seemed like my torturers had a sixth sense about it and knew I was going somewhere. When I came back from L.A. the second time, the girls took it beyond normal bullying.* These were big, tough girls. I was scrawny and short. They were fully capable of doing me bodily harm. As if they weren't already scary enough, then they sent me a note threatening me if I showed up in the cafeteria at lunch the next day. I'm not going to give any bullies out there ideas by saying exactly what they threatened. Let's just say it wasn't nice. And I know it sounds kind of silly and clichéd to be scared of a little note. You just have to trust

*can bullying be normal?

me. These girls weren't messing around.

I'd been trying to handle the bullying all by myself this whole time. I didn't want to show my fear, not to those girls or to my friends or to my parents. I never cried.* I didn't tell my parents. I tried everything I could think of. Sometimes I tried to defend myself. Sometimes I apologized. Sometimes I just walked away. I always felt alone. But the night I got the cafeteria threat it seemed like Operation Make Miley Miserable was escalating to a new level. More like Operation Take Miley Down. I was so scared that I told a friend from cheerleading about it on the phone. Should I pretend to have the flu? Should I skip lunch? Should I arm myself with a ketchup bottle and prepare for battle?

As soon as I hung up the phone, my dad came into the room. He sat down on the foot of my bed and told me he had overheard my conversation. I rolled my eyes. Dad wanted to know what was going on. I showed him the note, and told him I was pretty much scared out of my mind. Still I begged him not to do anything. I knew if he told my mom, she'd call the principal. She's that kind of mom. If she called the principal, that was

*in public, at least.

The mean girls were rubbing off on me, I guess.

46

it. They'd destroy me. Dad listened, and said he understood. But then he added, "You know I gotta tell Mom."

I followed Dad straight to Mom and said, "Mom, I will never speak to you again if you say anything." But I could see from their faces that as soon as I went to bed, they were going to have a Conversation.

I went to lunch the next day, unsure of where the Conversation had ended. What else could I do? If I hid from the girls today, they'd just get me tomorrow. **It was like an afterschool special about the runty girl who gets beat up. But instead of having a happy ending with an uplifting message about overcoming adversity, this plot would end with my living out the rest of my days a twelve-year-old hermit, friendless and alone.**

As soon as I sat down at my empty table in the loser boondocks of the lunchroom, three girls strutted up and stood towering over me. My stomach churned. I clutched my grilled cheese sandwich like it was the hand of my best friend. It pretty much *was* my best friend those days. I was done for.

They started cussing me and telling me to get up. *You know, like "Get up and fight!" Aaagh!*

I sat there, frozen. I didn't know what to do. I looked over and saw the mother of one of the girls sitting at a nearby table. A mother! And she was laughing.*

Finally, I couldn't take it anymore. I wasn't a chicken. What could they do to me? I was surrounded by people. I stood up, still a foot shorter than they were, and said, "What's your problem? What did I ever do to you?"

Before they could say or do anything, the principal walked in and interrupted, saying, "Girls!" That one word from the principal and all the kids in the lunchroom went "Ooohh."* Talk about embarrassing—and relieving!

*As in: "You're all in big trouble."

It turns out that after the Conversation, Mom had gone ahead and called the principal. At first my mom had thought it wasn't that big a deal, girls will be girls or whatever, but Dad had told her, "You never know. Things happen in schools all the time." Of course, that got my mom freaked out. And when it came down to it, I guess I was pretty relieved that my mom had stepped in.* I honestly don't know what those girls would have done to me, even with one of their mothers watching it all go down. The principal

*Let's keep that between us, though.

48

brought us into her office and forced us to "make up." As if we'd been in a two-sided argument about who stole whose pencil, when we all knew perfectly well that this was a straightforward case of torturing the innocent.

Only three girls were picking on me that day in the cafeteria, but I got a sense that the other kids enjoyed the show. I'd always gotten some teasing for having a well-known father. Classmates would say, "Your dad's a one-hit wonder. You'll never amount to anything— just like him." I just ignored it. I thought of him as successful and happy with his life. Maybe they thought I was snotty for being proud of my dad (well, he *is* the most amazing man ever), or for wanting to be my own person, or for wanting to be an actress and a singer. Maybe they just smelled insecurity. Maybe that was why they singled me out. Whatever the reason, to this day I still don't know what it was. I probably never will, and at this point I don't want to.

I don't really blame my former best friend, Rachel,* for betraying me. She was never outright mean to me. Honestly, I think they bullied her into dropping me and ignoring me. I like to think I

* Again, names have been changed!

wouldn't have ditched a friend the way she did, but I have a feeling she was as scared of her new friends as I was—the difference being that she was scared from *inside* the group and I was scared from *outside*.

I always find comfort, guidance, and answers in my faith. I turned to my Bible then as I often do now, and found this Psalm.

Psalm 25: 1-2, 5-7

O LORD, I GIVE MY LIFE TO YOU
I TRUST IN YOU, MY GOD.
DO NOT LET ME BE DISGRACED,
OR LET MY ENEMIES REJOICE IN MY DEFEAT.

LEAD ME BY YOUR TRUTH AND TEACH ME,
FOR YOU ARE THE GOD WHO SAVES ME.
ALL DAY LONG I PUT MY HOPE IN YOU.
REMEMBER O LORD, YOUR COMPASSION
    AND UNFAILING LOVE,
WHICH YOU HAVE SHOWN FROM LONG AGES PAST.

After the talk with the principal, the biggest threat was over, but I was still alone. And after bailing too many times for auditions, I didn't even have the comfort of cheerleading anymore. I just got by. I started hanging out with some older kids and tried to put it out of my mind, but the bully girls continued to give me a hard time every day. I hated school. I never turned my back to open my locker without being aware of who else was in the hall. I never lingered between classes or after school. Every time I went to the bathroom or walked around the corner, I was on edge. I didn't feel safe.

The Bottom of the Ocean

Remember Lyric and Melody? Trapped in their bowl? Well, one of the fish died. I'm pretty sure it was Melody. I was upset. I know—weird to get that distraught over something you can't even pet, but fish were my thing. Then my mom got me another fish. I should have named him Dissonance. He promptly ate Lyric.* After that, fish weren't my thing anymore. I had had enough with the strong picking on the weak.

* A harsh blow!

My perfect fishies were gone, but they taught me something lasting. Since then any time I want to write a song, I tell myself, *Think outside the bowl.* It's

a reminder to push myself, not to get stuck—not to see the world outside through a glass cage.

"Bottom of the Ocean" started off as a song about Lyric and Melody. But once I began writing, it was about so much more than my silly fish.* It was about anyone's dreams, boyfriends, a lost parent, an abusive relationship. It's saying if there's someone you've loved but for some reason you can't love them anymore, you have to take your feelings, scoop them out, and put them at the bottom of the ocean. Hide them there, carefully and respectfully, in the one place where they can't ever be found. "Bottom of the Ocean" is a "good-bye" song, a love song. You'd never think it was about fish. Well, except for the "ocean" part.

My friends turned into my enemies, even my best friend. I had no idea why I was the one they hated or what I could do to make it all better. I didn't fit any-where. Where does it all go? All the respect, all the friendship, all the love? I was powerless, lost, just kind of floating, and there was no end in sight. So I did what I talk about in "Bottom of the Ocean." I put all the losses and pain and fear someplace where no

✳ No offense to the fish. RIP

And if you're
wondering
about
Dissonance—
he's long down
the toilet.

one would find them again, down at the bottom of my own personal ocean.

And then I got the final call about *Hannah Montana*.

Peace out,
suckers!

The Call

BROKEN GLASS

Have you ever felt like you need to start over,
Be a new person and be set free?
Sometimes, do you ever feel
As if you're looking through broken glass
With a broken future and shattered past?
Don't let the what-ifs or should've-beens
*   hold you back.*
It's your time and your dreams.
Be a sun shining bright
Not a cloud dull and dim.
You can change the world
And bring the light.

Not to sound like Susie Sunshine, but it just goes to show, when you are ready to move on or if you come to peace with pain, you'll find a silver lining. Mine came in the form of a phone call.

I was on my cell* with Patrick, one of my oldest friends. He and I had just discovered iTunes, and he was playing some song off his computer for me. Actually, it was "I Can't Take It" by Tegan and Sara. I'll never forget it. My mom was nearby in the kitchen and answered the landline when it rang. She screamed so loudly I thought someone had died. Then, a moment later, she started yelling, "You got it! You got it!"

"It" was Hannah. It's a strange and amazing feeling to get exactly what you want. It doesn't happen very often, so when it does, your brain is kind of like, *Whoa, hold on, what's the catch?* It's tempting to dwell on what the downside might be or how much suddenly has to get done. But seeing my mom all happy and jumping—yes, my mom was jumping— I finally had to accept that this was just plain good. I told my brain to just be quiet. This was awesome! I had a part! A character that I loved! I'd get to sing *and* act. It was too perfect. As reality sank in, I started

* My parents caved and got me some minutes.

jumping and screaming too. Poor Patrick was left hanging on the other end of the phone. He must have thought a tornado was destroying our home.

The whole morning—my mom answering the phone and screaming that I got the part—makes it sound like I bought a ticket and won the lottery, simple as that. But now you know it was more like a slow-motion lottery, during which there were plenty of opportunities for pain, suffering, and one way-too-long trip to the bathroom. I'll never forget how it felt to be that girl. You know the one. That friendless girl who sits alone in the cafeteria every day and is clearly just trying to survive, but the other kids go out of their way to pick on her anyway, and half of you feels bad for not doing anything to stop it, but the other half of you is just really, really relieved it's not you sitting there? That was me. And it was awful.

Getting the part did change everything, suddenly and irreversibly. I was moving forward and leaving the past behind, but I didn't dare forget the struggle. There was a reason for it. I brought that girl with me, and she reminds me to be compassionate. To not hold grudges. To be supportive. To be there for others when I know I'm needed. My dad likes to remind me of Newton's third law of motion—that for every action there is an equal and opposite reaction. For all I'd struggled during that year, for all the hours I sat alone at lunch or retreated to my room, writing songs, there was a balance. A balance in my life, just like there is a balance in the world.

For every action there is an equal and opposite reaction. You never know what it's going to look like on the other side, but you'll see it eventually if you keep your eyes open.

I really believe that.

Here it was—one single phone call that was more than payback for sixth-grade hell. The jumping. The screaming. The madness. (Dad just said, "See? I told you. It's meant for you.") I had flown to Los Angeles to audition and/or meet with Disney executives at least four times. I had been too small for the part. I had been too young for the part. They wanted someone taller. Or someone older. Or someone with a better singing voice. Or someone with more acting chops. Or someone with all of the above. They had tried really hard to find anybody other than me for the part. I'd been working and hoping for Hannah and warding off a pack of (well, three) teenage bullies that whole sucky year of sixth grade. I was eleven when I first auditioned. Now, after a year, I really was twelve.* Now, amazingly, incredibly, impossibly, the part was mine.

*Still not very big, but . . .

This had been my dream for about as long as I could remember. But oddly enough, now that it was actually happening, my excitement wasn't so much about what I'd achieved and where I was going. It was about escaping. I wasn't thinking, "Great! I've got a part in a Disney show! I finally landed something! I'm going to be a big star!" *Hannah Montana* should have been something I was running to, but instead it was an excuse to run *away* from what had been the worst year of my life. I was determined to get out of Nashville before starting high school. So when I got that call, it felt like God saving me from an impossible situation. My first thought (after the screaming, crazy, holy heck one, of course) was, *I'm outta here!*

Chloe Stewart

Can you imagine being bullied by your classmates, not even having a best friend, then moving to Hollywood and getting to audition crowds of eager girls who want to play your best friend on a TV show? The *yeah rock* would-be Lilly I had tried out with months earlier—the dark-haired one I'd hurried to change out of my Dr Pepper—stained skirt to meet?—I never saw that Lilly again.

While the new potential Lillys were trying out, my mom got friendly with some of the casting people. They joked about my dad being a hunk. And my mom joked about how they should bring him out here to play my dad on the show. And then (as my mom tells it) everyone was like, "Wait, seriously?"

My mom sat me down at the kitchen table to talk about it. I loved the idea of having Daddy around, but I was worried that if he got the part, people would think that he'd been cast first and I'd been hired because of him.* Dad worried about the same thing. He said, "This part is meant for you. What if I mess it up?"

*After all my hard work!

But we all really wanted to find a way for our whole family to be together. Dad had been in Canada for so long. He was always traveling back and forth. If the show was successful and they decided to make it into a series, then I'd have to move to L.A. Would we uproot the whole family? How was it all going to work? That's when Mom said, "Well, we've talked a lot about how Hannah Montana is meant for you. What if Hannah's dad is meant for Billy Ray?" We decided to leave it up to fate.

They had already narrowed it down to two potential dads for me—or rather, Hannah Montana. Now they added Dad to the mix. He came in, took one look at the other dad actors, pointed at the best-looking one, and told the producers, "Hire that dude. Make my daughter's show a hit." But then they called him in to read lines with me.

Sitting at the conference table with him was completely surreal. I mean, he's my dad! We were joking around and laughing together. We did our handshake, which is very complicated and silly. We sang together—I think it was my dad's song "I Want My Mullet Back." My mom was out in the waiting room with the two other dads. She says you could hear me saying, "Dad, that isn't the line!" and everyone rolling with laughter. But apparently it was during "I Want My Mullet Back" that the other dads looked at each other and said, "We're doomed."

And they were right. Dad got the part. We'd been praying for a way to keep the family together, and here was the crazy, completely unexpected solution. We'd deal with rumors of who got what part first later. For now, we were just psyched to be in the same country!

Dad's being cast was great. But the rest of the characters had been determined, and now I had other castmates too. Chloe Stewart (Hannah's alter ego) had a brother, Jackson (Jason Earles). And she had best friends, Lilly (Emily Osment) and Oliver (Mitchel Musso). And to be perfectly honest—in the beginning, I was intimidated by all of them. Emily had been in tons of commercials, TV shows, and the movie *Spy Kids*. Mitchel had been in a couple of TV shows and movies, including *Life Is Ruff*, which was Disney, so he knew the drill. I had done, um, a few episodes of my dad's show *Doc*, which was a drama, and a couple of lines in a movie. Once—in Alabama. I'd never done any comedy whatsoever. **So there I was trying to be funny and act and sing and dance and look cool and make it clear that my dad hadn't gotten me the part, and attempting to befriend my costars while wearing Hannah's cheap blond wig half the time.** And guess what?—in no time, it all felt easier and much more natural than sitting in that sixth-grade cafeteria.

Oh, and about Chloe Stewart. Doesn't ring a bell, does it? There's a reason. You see, my real name is Destiny Hope Cyrus.* Everybody called me Miley. My character's name was Chloe Stewart. Her alter ego's name was Hannah Montana. It was just way too many names. So they dropped the one that was easiest to let go. My character's name changed to Miley Stewart.

* More on that later . . .

And people still get confused. I'm not confused. I'm Miley in real life. I'm Miley on my show (except when I'm Hannah). The only place I'm *not* Miley is on my original birth certificate, which is now defunct since I had my name legally changed. And when that glorious day comes, my driver's license will say Miley.

Hannah Who?

While we were taping the pilot, Disney let me know that there was just, ah, one more tiny little thing they wanted me to do. A concert.* That's right—they wanted me to perform a concert as Hannah Montana in front of a crowd of people who had no idea who I was, *before* the show had even started.** When the big night came, I was a nervous wreck. Sure, I'd been backstage, even onstage with my dad at plenty of concerts. But now there were new songs, new choreography, new dancers, props, and wardrobe changes. And no Dad. The focus was all on me.

The crowd at Glendale Centre Theatre—not far from the Disney studios—didn't know who or what they were going to see. They just knew they were

* yikes!

** Double yikes!

watching an unknown girl named Hannah Montana, and she had something to do with a new Disney show. And it was free. I'm sure some of those people wish they could travel in time and scalp those free tickets for big bucks.

Not that I approve of that behavior!

I couldn't believe anyone showed up at the concert. Who wanted to see an unknown singer? When I started, I was scared that I would tank—and I felt stupid for pretending to be such a hotshot star when nobody knew who I was. It was so weird. Between songs, I'd whisper into the mike, "I'll be right back," and scurry off the stage like a little mouse to ask my mom and the producers if I was doing okay.

Then, around when I was singing "Pumping Up the Party Now," I noticed that people were into it. They seemed excited to see the show. It gave me a second to pause (in my head—I kept singing, of course) and realize what was happening to me. It didn't matter how odd and contrived this performance was. I thought to myself, *I'm happy to be here. I really am.* That was it. After that moment I started to get into my groove. I found out later that Gary Marsh, an exec at Disney Channel, turned to my mom and said, "Didn't take her long to settle in."

By the end of the concert the audience was standing up, cheering, shouting "Han-nah! Han-nah! Han-nah!" I ran across the front of the stage. I high-fived them. I improvised. I just had fun. **It was really happening. This was my moment.**

Some of that concert is still used in the show, sort of as if it's Hannah's music video. They use the footage from "Pumping Up the Party Now," with me in my pajamas,* in the opening sequence and to promote the show sometimes.

And then the pilot was done, and they slapped braces on my teeth.

annah
as
grown
up so
much—
she'd never
perform in
sleepover
PJ's now!

Losing Pappy

Before I get back to the braces, I want to talk about Pappy. While we were taping the pilot, Dad was flying back and forth between the set of *Hannah Montana* and my pappy's bedside. Pappy was my grandfather on my dad's side. He was sick, really sick with lung cancer, but all the amazing memories I have of him were in my head as I worked. I knew he wanted me to follow this dream.

Pappy had a log cabin in Cave Run, Kentucky. It is the most beautiful place on earth. In the morning, he'd make bacon for us and tell some crazy story about what the dogs were up to or what the neighbors said.

Each of us kids had a room upstairs in his cabin. Whenever we came to visit, I'd head up to my room the first night and he'd have positioned an old bearskin rug flat on the floor with its head popping up. It scared me to death every time. But that was Pappy for you. I loved his teasing. I even loved the way Pappy smelled. He wore the same deodorant for years—it's a generic country brand—and now I keep it around because it reminds me of him.

We spent plenty of time in that cabin, just goofing around. I would change the outgoing message on the answering machine to say "Hey, thanks for calling my pappy," and then I would blow a whistle that sounded like a train—*whoo whoo whoo*—and say, "I love him and hope you love him too." (If you'd known him you would have.)

The cabin was near a mountain that had a cave. During the day, Pappy would help me, Brazz, and Trace (my sister Noah wasn't born yet) look for arrowheads and scout for bats. Pappy was a giant kid. When we'd go fishing,* Pappy would drive ahead of us in his old-man car and my dad would follow behind, driving way too slow, never able to keep up. Dad is usually a cautious driver (except when he's behind the wheel of a dirt bike or a four-wheeler).

* well, . . . at least I went along until I got my foot stuck in a hole on the bridge and they had to cut me out before the catfish ate my toes. After that I wasn't so into fishing.

7 things my Pappy used to say

1. the more you stomp in poo, the more it stinks.

2. persistence is to the quality of the character of man what carbon is to steel.

3. good for the goose, good for the gander.

4. wherever you go . . . there ya are.

5. a trying time is no time to quit trying.

6. you're as full of poop as a christmas turkey. =)

& my favorite one . . . 7. I love you.

Pappy had a husky voice like me and a stomach that always stuck out a little—like he'd just had a big meal. He was always spouting folk wisdom that made no sense to some people, but it did to me (usually). If I was talking about someone who made me angry, he'd say, "The more you stomp in poo, the more it stinks," or "When you knock 'em out, you don't need no judge." (That's what he always told my dad because he used to be a boxer.) When I was wearing something—say, a hat—I'd say, "Don't you like my hat, Pappy?" If he didn't like it he'd say, "Oh, sure, I'd like to have two of them. One to crap on and the other to cover it up with." Then my dad would chime in, "Yeah, me too." And I'd say, "I have no clue what either one of you is talking about." It didn't matter, though. He was just the best granddad I can imagine.

Pappy was always a good audience. The staircase in his cabin led to an upstairs loft, and when I was a little kid—five or six—I'd put on a show, belting out "Tomorrow" from *Annie* as I came down the stairs. Pappy would clap and whistle and say, "Go on up there and do it again." I ate it up. And when I was at the cabin, I always played his piano. I never took piano lessons, but I liked—and still like—letting my fingers tinkle around the keys. Pappy called that tinkling "The Rain Song."

That's how I ended up writing the song "I Miss You" for Pappy. He was so sick. I knew he was dying, and slowly so did my heart. I couldn't imagine life without him. It was the hardest song for me to write. I was working on it with my mom's good friend Wendi, and it was just killing me. Finally I said, "I can't write anymore. I gotta stop." But I knew what my heart wanted to say, and whatever's in my heart finds its way to my fingertips. So we pushed on and finished the song. I really wanted Pappy to hear "I Miss You" before he died. I never got to sing it for him, but toward the end my dad played Pappy a quick cut of the song, and I like to believe that it gave him hope, like he continues to give me hope.

Pappy said he refused to die before *Hannah Montana* aired on TV for the first time, but he passed away two days before the premiere. Still, he did get to see a tape of the pilot. I know he was proud.

In the South, funerals are like weddings. Everyone shows up in big hats to gossip and pay their respects. It's practically a family reunion. At Pappy's funeral I couldn't see anything but my granddad. There was an open casket and I wanted to touch his hand one last time, to say good-bye. But I didn't want to remember him that way, so I stayed back. That moment still haunts me.

After Pappy died, I kept circling around his death. If you've lost a grandparent, maybe you know how that goes. I missed him. I still do. I mourned him. I still do. I kept thinking about how I promised I'd let him take my older sister Brandi and me to King's Island (an amusement park), but never got a chance. I got stuck on the times I didn't talk to him on the phone. There was a voice mail from Pappy saved on our answering machine, and I listened to it over and over again, because every time it brought him back as if he'd never left.

Then I had a dream. It was Pappy, wanting me to move on. He said, "I can't leave with you holding on so tightly. You can't let my death stop your life." When I woke up, his voice was so alive in my head it was as if he'd just said good-bye and walked out the door. Out of habit, I went to the phone to listen to his voice mail. It was gone. Deleted. Floating away out into the ether. As though Pappy was telling me to let go.

My dad has taken over Pappy's tendency to talk in gibberish. He'll say "What's good for the goose is good for the gander." The other day he said "spigot" instead of "faucet," and the way he said it was just like Pappy: "spicket." And I finally saw that it doesn't matter if I let go of Pappy. He'll always be with us.

Believe

Just because they shot a pilot—the first episode of the show—didn't mean *Hannah Montana* would ever see the light of day. Lots of executives had to decide if it was good enough. If they approved it, then they'd "pick it up." That meant we'd make more episodes, and the show would go on the air. Which was what we all wanted.

We were back in Nashville when the news came that *Hannah Montana* had been picked up for thirteen episodes. Disney wanted me in L.A. in seven days. Seven days! My mom didn't want to uproot the whole family so quickly without putting us in a place that would feel like a home. She didn't want the move to be hard or to feel like a sacrifice for my brothers and sisters. My mom is like that. She isn't the type to get caught up in Hollywood or the idea of my being a star. She always thinks about the big picture. The whole family. How we can be stable and normal. Mom went online and bought the smallest house in La Cañada she could find. Just like that. As if it were a T-shirt from a catalogue. Mom is so twenty-first century.

Literally.

One of the first things we did when we arrived in L.A. was to go to the Disney offices to say thank you. We had lunch with my agents, then drove in a convertible to Disney. My dad and I always rode four-wheelers around our farm, redneck style. This was the opposite end of the top-down experience. Wasn't I glamorous in my convertible? A TV star, on her way to thank the producers. Except when I walked into Gary Marsh's office, a look of horror crossed his face. "What happened to you?" he asked. Riding in the convertible had ~~messed up~~* my hair. Which was dyed a weird blond color. I'd had two teeth pulled. And oh yeah, the braces. I had braces. It was not a pretty sight. I got off my high horse pretty fast.

*restyled

The hair went back to brown. The braces came off. I got a little retainer with fake teeth to fill in the holes

I called it
my flipper.

while my grown-up teeth grew in. That was my first perk as a TV star: having an excuse to ditch the braces.

After they "fixed" me, there was still more to accomplish before we started shooting the series. They had to do my wardrobe. I had go into a studio to record music for the whole first season. Oh, and they had to fit me for wigs. The pilot wig was a joke. Now I would get real, expensive wigs that were molded to my head. If you've never experienced a wig fitting, let me tell you—it's not very glamorous. They put you in a wig cap, which is like a swimming cap made of stocking; Having a wig they put Scotch tape all around it until it's a hard made: every form; then they use that to make a mold. girl's dream!

Wigs done, the series got rolling. Soon after, there was a party at the set for the premiere of the show. Emily and I both wore black dresses. We were so excited to watch the final version of the pilot—the version that millions of viewers would watch on Disney Channel. We hoped.

The show was far better than I expected it to be. You say a line six times, sixty times, and you end up with no idea which one they'll pick in the editing room, how it will sound, and how you'll look saying it.

You sing a song in a studio and only imagine how it will come out with sound production and lip-synching. But there we were, up on screen. Me, Dad, and all my new friends. I have to say, I thought we were pretty awesome. No matter what happened, that moment was mine, and I will never let it go.

The very next day I went to an amusement park with my aunt. We weren't thinking about the show. We had no idea what the ratings were. It didn't occur to us that people had actually seen my face on television the night before. We were on our way to the roller coaster, when six thirteen-year-old girls ran up to me and asked me for my autograph.* I did an internal roundoff–back handspring–backflip for joy! "Sure!" I said, so hyperenthusiastically that I'm pretty sure I scared my very first fans (who were taller than I was). That was the moment when I realized that *Hannah Montana* wasn't just a new job that I loved. There were people out there watching us. Real people, who recognized me on the street. I wasn't just Miley Cyrus anymore. I was carrying Miley Stewart and Hannah Montana around with me. It was weird. It was cool. I was twelve.

* No lie!

Haven't you practiced your signature in school notebooks or when you're talking on the phone? I have. Page after page where I should have been taking notes is covered with my name, accompanied by all different doodles and flourishes. I knew how to sign my name, but what else did I want to tell these girls, my first fans? I thought back to what I would have wanted to hear when I was just one of fifty Hannah Montana wannabes sitting nervously in a waiting room. I thought back to what I would have wanted to hear when I was crouched alone in the school bathroom, at the end of my rope. I thought back to what my fish would have wanted to hear after his best friend bit the dust. Now I knew exactly what I wanted to write. I took a long time with those first six signatures, making sure I did them perfectly.

Believe

Miley Cyrus

MILE TWO
Two Worlds

Amazing Grace

Well, I think I'm ready to go back to the very beginning now. It's tough to remember so far back when you're an old, wise broad like me, but here I go. Waaay back.

I know that it seems like I took the whole Hannah thing in stride. Don't think I wasn't completely over the moon. But I also had an advantage. As a little girl, I had had my fair share of the spotlight. When I was tiny, I was my dad's shadow. He kind of got used to having me around. So when he went on the road to play concerts—my dad was always a singer, this acting thing came later—he wanted me with him as much as possible. And he was in the fast lane for a while there. I sat on his shoulders in front of thousands of people.

I rode helicopters, Lear jets, buses, and limos. Sometimes he'd bring me onstage to sing "Hound Dog" with him, and I'm told they had some trouble getting me off. At the end of each show, when the fans gave him gifts, I'd run out in front of the cheering crowd, help my daddy gather up the flowers, home-made bracelets, and bras, and then we'd go straight to a hospital to donate them. Except the bras. They made excellent hammocks for my dolls.

When I was all of two years old, my dad brought me along to an Elvis Presley tribute. Priscilla and Lisa Marie Presley had organized the event—which was being taped live for television—at the Pyramid, a 20,000-seat arena in Memphis. It was an all-star lineup: Aretha Franklin, the Jordanaires, Eddie Rabbitt, Bryan Adams, the Sweet Inspirations, Tony Bennett, all singing Elvis songs. Dad's turn came in the middle of the show. He sang "One Night with You" while I watched from backstage with Mammie in my frilly little party dress. Then, for the grand finale, Dad started singing "Amazing Grace," and all the other singers came to join him onstage one by one.

It was a bluesy, rock 'n' roll, Memphis-style

rendition of "Amazing Grace." I can't really say whether I remember the moment, or whether it's been told to me so many times that I feel like I remember it, but finally I couldn't hold back any longer. I broke away from Mammie and ran out onto the stage. As Daddy tells it, the Sweet Inspirations just scooped me up and held me high, looking out at the audience. **There I was, taking it all in, feeling the spirit of that song, the music, and Elvis as much as anyone—in front of thousands of people!**

The Sweet Inspirations passed me to the Jordanaires, who passed me to Eddie Rabbitt. (Sort of like the famous-singer version of hot potato.) I was waving at the audience the whole time, loving it. The last person to hold me was Tony Bennett. (Sort of like the famous singer getting stuck with the hot potato.) At the end of the song, he brought me back to Dad, looked him straight in the eyes, and said, "You've got a special little girl here." When Dad tells this story,[*] he says that Tony Bennett said it like he meant it. Like he was really saying, *Man, she's got something really special. A certain charisma.*

Two-year-old interrupting live TV = big no-no!

[*] like, every day

84

She connects with people. That's my dad for you. Always embellishing his stories in my favor.

I don't know what to say about Tony Bennett, but what I do know is that I wasn't a bit afraid of the stage. I was with my daddy, I dug the music, and I felt like I belonged there—as if the stage was a puzzle, and I was a missing piece that fit right in. Or maybe I was the puzzle, and being onstage was a missing piece of me. Okay, let's just say I felt a lot more comfortable being up onstage than I do now trying to make up analogies!

Hunting Rabbits

My earliest music memories aren't all on stage. As early as I can remember, music was part of my everyday life. Pappy's father, my great-grandfather (E. L. Cyrus), was a Pentecostal preacher. On top of being a legislator for the state of Kentucky, Pappy (Ronald Ray Cyrus) sang with the Crownsmen for a time and always had a gospel quartet. My dad's mother (Ruthie Cyrus) was also musical. She sang and played piano by ear. And when it came to our house, Dad's guitar was always out. He, my uncle, and my Pappy would sing "Little Red Caboose" or "Silent Night." Especially around Christmas, the house was full of carols.

When I was growing up, Dad brought home lots of

his musician friends. I sat on Waylon Jennings's lap while he sang "Good-Hearted Woman." When I was ten or eleven, Ed King* showed me the chords for "Sweet Home Alabama" on my first guitar.

*The Lynyrd Skynyrd guitarist. How cool is that?

Music is the love of my life. It's a total escape from reality. Music transports you to another place, someplace unexpected and meaningful.

One day Johnny Neel* came to visit. Daddy and I took a walk with him up to the top of a hill near our house. Johnny was blind, so we walked carefully. He used a cane while I held his other hand. When we sat down at the top, Johnny said, "It must be so beautiful up here. I wish I could see how beautiful it is." This happened before I can remember, but according to Dad, I said, "Just listen to the wind. You can hear God's voice in the wind." And when Johnny Neel just sat there quietly, I said, "Put your head down close to the grass so you can hear it." He got down on all fours, put his ear to the ground, and said, "You're right, baby."

*A former keyboardist for the Allman Brothers.

Dad = wrapped around my finger.

My dad tells all these stories about me and his

musician friends. But my favorite is the one about Carl Perkins.* Carl Perkins brought his rabbit hunting dogs over from Memphis to walk around the farm with Dad. Dad and Carl weren't really hunting. They just liked to watch the dogs trail the rabbits. I was six years old, but I went with them. I always went with them.

So Carl's dogs were walking through the field, they caught the scent of a rabbit, and they took off into the hollow. Carl looked down at me and said, "Now, honey, I want you to remember this day. Me and your dad, we ain't carrying no guns, but we love rabbit hunting. Always remember that rabbit hunting is just like the music business." That made no sense to me. "What do you mean?" I asked. He said, "It's not about killing the rabbit. It's about enjoying the chase." Daddy says that the dogs were howling, and we were standing there—him, me, and Carl Perkins, and he remembers that moment like it was yesterday. I'm not sure I remember it quite that clearly, but I know that day is still with me.

No single one of those encounters made me who I am. Not one of them convinced me to be an actor or a musician. But our hours and days add up. Little moments attach themselves to other little moments and collect into big dreams. A sunset, a walk, a few small words of wisdom. **We become what we experience.**

Hannah and Lilly

Maybe my childhood experiences did have a little something to do with getting the part on *Hannah Montana*, but none of my dad's friends gave me any nuggets of wisdom about life on the set with my costars. If a TV show is like its own little world, then, in the beginning, the kids on our show were like an entire junior high school class. There was jealousy. There were fights. There was friendship. There was love. The only thing that was different: there were only three of us.

Emily, Mitchel, and I are all close in age. Three is never a good number. At any given point, someone's going to feel like a third wheel—that's just the way threes work. Mitchel and I were sort of insta-best

Dad, Mom, and me
as a newborn.
What a family!

The only way Dad got me to eat
veggies—he had to strap me down
in the high chair.

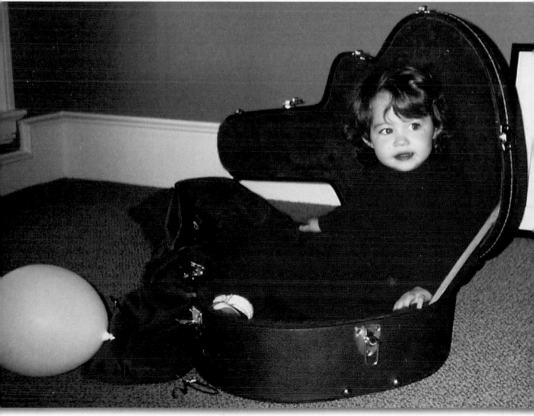

My own little music box. Sometimes I wish I could still fit.

Dad's jet: Living the
rock star life at age 2,
hanging with my
two #1 fans: Dad and
Mammie.

 PAPPY, my hero!

Trace and Brandi; me, Braison, and Dad: tranquility.

I'm two!

Me and my best friend, Willie Nelson. I pushed him everywhere in that stroller.

Here I am with Trace (No. 2) at a baseball game. He hit me in the head with a bat L8r that day. (By accident, of course!)

Destiny Hope Cyrus: Student of the month. Mommy was so proud.

So cool!

Mommy + me at a cheerleading competition.

I fell off that wall later!

Me and Noah:
who's who?

Love

Passing the torc

A trip to Disneyland—
when I still had to
wait in line . . .
and pay.

Braison and me:
bad 2 the bone.

Family bonding!

Some of the best memories were made on that stage!

On my trip to L.A. for **pilot season** in 6th grade.

Life is speeding up. A moment behind the scenes.

connecting with my fans in NYC! So much fun!

friends. We're both crazy, silly, fun, high-energy, joking around with no real filters on what we say or do. We even had a little case of puppy love for a while there. It was sweet.

Meanwhile, Emily's more reserved. Also, she's beautiful and athletic. There was competition between us—girls struggle with that, and we were no exception. I didn't do much to fix it. I mean, I wanted to, but I had no idea how to go about fixing it. I never got along with girls as well as I did with guys. Hadn't I just endured Operation Make Miley Miserable, which was an all-girl campaign, for a year?

Emily and I tried to be friends, we really did, but it always ended in a fight. We're just so different. She's from L.A.—I'm from the South. She's opinionated. I'm not opinionated . . . but I'm so not opinionated that I'm opinionated about *not* being opinionated. She's supersmart. I felt dumb. Once in our classroom on set we got into a huge yelling argument after the teacher left. It was so bad, and we were so upset, that we each went home and told our parents. Both families all sat down together and tried to work it out. After those peace talks, we tiptoed around each other for a couple of weeks, but it didn't last. Soon enough we were back at each other's throats.

Usually on set everyone's mellow if someone flubs a line. Not us. We'd be, like, "Gosh," and roll our eyes in exasperation if the other one messed up. As soon as a take was over, I'd say, "Are we done with this scene now?" or she'd say, "Can we go?" There was no warmth, no chemistry. We were playing BFs, and neither of us wanted to be there. Finally the producers said, "You two have to pull it together." I think sometimes people forget how old we are. They wonder why we're behaving the way we do. The pettiness. The drama. The acne depression—I'll get to that later. We're teenagers! Our job is to fight. That's gotta be the downside of making a TV show about teenagers. You have to work with teenagers. On the upside . . . hmm. Maybe there isn't an upside.

I really wanted to be best friends with Emily. My dad was playing my dad. Jason Earles, who plays Jackson, was like a big brother to me. The show felt real to me, and I wanted my relationship with Lilly to feel real too. I knew it didn't have to—show business is show business—but I was disappointed. There were times when I didn't think we could ever be friends. We just couldn't figure out how to get along.

SPOTLIGHT ON YOU
written for Emily

I am tryin' to be brave
Prayin' everything's gonna go okay
'Cuz I know I'm 'bout to be in . . .
The spotlight
I see myself up on that stage
With the spotlight
With the cheerin' crowd before my eyes
Rockin' on my guitar
Bein' a superstar
But all I really need is YOU

Time went on, and the three of us—me, Mitchel, and Emily—were stuck together. So we stuck together. And over time we found ways to genuinely bond. There was a narrow wooden catwalk up above the set. We called it the "C.A.D." room.* Getting up to the C.A.D. room was precarious. It was several stories

* C.A.D.= inside joke.

high! You had to hang on to a bar or you'd fall down to certain death. The producers must have been glad to have us out of their hair. They didn't care where we went: "We don't see anything. We don't know anything. This isn't on us," was their attitude.

We'd sneak up there for lunch, and for an hour it felt like we were hiding out in a treehouse, high above our jobs and homework and parents. We were all in the same situation—we had a great opportunity. It meant working like grown-ups, but it wasn't always easy to behave like grown-ups. Witness my spats with Emily. But up in the C.A.D. room we got to be normal, mischievous kids for a change. The pressure was off, and there were even hints of fondness between Emily and me. Our characters got along so well. Why couldn't we act the same in real life? For all our troubles, deep down I ~~think~~* we loved each other, even then. But we had a long way to go before we'd *know really be friends.

Daddy's Little Buddy

Meanwhile, Dad and I were working really well together. Every teenager and father have some of the same problems. You want a new phone, but your dad doesn't want to give you the money to buy it. Your dad won't let you go to a movie because you need to stay home and study. You get jealous when your dad starts writing songs with the Jonas Brothers. (Okay, maybe that last one isn't exactly universal.)

The *Hannah Montana* writers were coming up with stories about stuff that made sense in my relationship with my dad because they were normal teenager/parent struggles. But as they watched us, they picked up on our dynamic and used that to make the characters even more like us. Like Dad calling me "Bud" on the show. He always calls me "Little Buddy" and "Bud" in real life. And some of that real Southern stuff comes straight from my dad's mouth, like "Dang flabbit." That is so Dad.

They also found ways to use some of my dad's songs in the show. "Ready, Set, Don't Go" is a song that Dad wrote when I first got the Hannah part. He hadn't been cast yet. The family had packed up and was heading to Los Angeles. He watched us drive away and felt happy to see my dreams coming true and sad at the idea of me going so far away—and growing up. What Dad doesn't have that bittersweet moment?

A year later, we would make an episode around that song. It was the highest rated of all the episodes that had aired so far, and "Ready, Set, Don't Go" became a hit song for us both. Of course, Dad wasn't thinking about any of that when he wrote the song. He was living his life, and he processes his emotions through music, just like me.

As time went on our lives overlapped more and more with our characters and vice versa. And that was fine by me.

On with the Show

I sort of expected to be nervous at my new job, but taping the show wasn't nearly as terrifying as auditioning had been. On set nobody was judging me. I wasn't standing in front of a group of people who would determine my future. Best of all, it wasn't live. If something didn't work, we could try again. There was always more tape. Sure, it still made me anxious sometimes. But this was where I wanted to be. I was working with a team, trying to make the best show we could.

From the beginning there were some surreal moments. For example, it was a little weird having people pick out boyfriends for me. I had nothing to do with the auditioning, so I'd just show up to work on

Monday and be introduced to my new boyfriend. *Oh, hi, there.* The kissing scenes—you'd think that would be awkward, kissing someone you barely know—but they just don't feel real. Neither person means it. It's the job. I just kiss the same way I'd pretend to sleepwalk or to gag at the sight of Jackson's closet. It's a stunt. Though I have to admit I was a little excited when I saw that Miley was going to kiss Jake. I thought Cody Linley was dreamy. And of course I loved it in season two when Jesse McCartney guest starred. I've been a fan of his forever.

Toward the end of that first season, superstars like Dolly Parton, Brooke Shields, and Vicki Lawrence came in to guest star. Maybe I should have been intimidated, but it was our show. They were visiting a place where my costars and I spent our lives. It was my comfort zone. Most of the time. Except when Miley Stewart had to parasail wearing a chicken costume. And later when I had to wear a Sumo wrestler fatsuit, I completely freaked out. I thought wearing a wig was bad, but those huge costumes gave me new respect for the people who wear Mickey Mouse suits at Disneyland. I could not handle that. I guess I get claustrophobic. I'm usually fine, but for those scenes I wanted my mom right there.

I got superlucky with *Hannah Montana*. From the very beginning, I felt like I *was* Hannah. I didn't really have to do anything to get into character or to try to feel what she felt. Those are skills that I developed later, but in the beginning, I just felt as though the part was written perfectly for me. Even learning lines was easy. I'm a freak of nature. I can read a scene twice and get it. Before I got the part, I never worried about my memorization skills (in hindsight I probably should have!), but it turned out I didn't need to. Sure, I still messed up a few times, but that was part of the learning process.

I was kind of the same way about rehearsing. Run lines? Practice? Not my favorite. My *favorite* days of the work week are the days when we actually film the show. I think of it as the real day, the real deal. Rehearsals feel like slow motion, molasses, compared to the adrenaline rush of performing.

All that aside, I wouldn't trade any of it, slow times and all. And in the very beginning, everything was so new that nothing felt remotely slow. I remember the first time I really got gussied up for the red carpet was for the premiere of *Chicken Little*. It was a Disney movie and I wanted to see it, so I asked for tickets to the premiere. Mom and I went shopping for a fancy dress at Charlotte Russe. I remember saying, "Mom, can't I tell them I have a premiere?" I thought they'd give me extra help or bring me a glass of sparkling water or something. Mom said, "No one's going to believe you. Do you know how many people in L.A. come into stores and say that?"

I ended up wearing a black blazer with a cross on it. I thought I was cute—but compared to what I get to wear these days . . . When we went to the movie I walked down the red carpet, toward all the flashing cameras and photographers yelling stars' names. "Zach! Joan! Steve!" When I strolled by, the cameras were lowered. There was silence. They had no idea who I was. So much for my red-carpet fantasy.

When the movie was over, Mom and I went to the after-party. Everyone was talking and mingling and *everyone* seemed to know each other. We got our plates of food and looked for a place to sit. All the tables were full of people who had obviously been in the business a lot longer than me. There was no place to sit. So we plopped down on the floor to eat. Nobody noticed us. We were the biggest losers in history. It was pretty humbling.

7 stars I'd like to work with

1. Hilary Duff
2. Jennifer Aniston
3. Meryl Streep
4. Shia LaBeouf
5. John Lennon (I don't care if he's dead)
6. Johnny Cash (ditto)
7. Elvis (OK—I love the dead guys)

The Spotlight

September 13, 2006

    This is the beginning and the end. The beginning of a long journey and a new path, and the end of an ordinary lifestyle. I hope I find love, adventure, fun, and excitement.

Despite my mouthful of humble pie, life kept going—full throttle. I went on tour, opening for The Cheetah Girls' The Party's Just Begun tour in the fall of 2006. We were done shooting the first season of *Hannah Montana*, but only half of it had aired on TV. Before The Cheetah Girls concert, nobody knew if folks would care that I was opening for them. True, *Hannah Montana* had been an instant success, but that didn't mean anybody wanted to see me in concert *as Hannah*. Hannah's a fictional singer. Maybe all her fame was fictional too. So the concert creators kept it cheap. There was no dramatic curtain, parting slowly to reveal me onstage. Nor did I rise up on a platform like a real rocker. So how *did* I appear onstage? Two dancers stood holding a plain white bed sheet up to hide me, then dropped it. That's right—a bed sheet. I had four dancers.* I had a band track instead of an actual band.** Hannah's costumes were all straight off the rack of Forever 21.*** But I didn't care if I was standing in front of a plain black wall. **My dad always says that a real musician can make a great show out of anything, no matter how small.** I was determined to be a great musician.

When you're the opening act, you figure nobody's there to see *you*. They come in with their friends; they're talking, goofing around, and getting psyched for the main act, and they have zero reason to pay any attention to that random girl in a blond wig who thinks she's a TV star. But this concert mattered a heck of a lot to me. It was my first and possibly only

* Now I'm up to twelve dancers.

** Now I have a seven person band.

*** Now all Hannah's clothes are custom-sewn.

chance to show everyone what I could do as a performer, and I couldn't afford to mess it up. I was supposed to get the crowd excited. If they weren't pumped when The Cheetah Girls came onstage, I'd be to blame.

No pressure!

7 things that keep me up at night

1. Sponge Bob
2. coffee beans
3. eating before bed
4. reading the Bible
5. playing the guitar
6. knowing I have to get up early
7. thinking about the past

The shows all sold out, which was a surprise to everyone. I liked a big audience. At least with that many people, I didn't have to worry that there'd be no applause, just crickets. I could handle the number of people—I hoped.

I'm never alone backstage. Before the show starts, my dancers and I have a little ritual. We gather in a circle with our hands together in the center and shout, "Pop off!"* Then my stage manager, Scottie Dog, a tattooed old-time rock 'n' roller, shows me where to wait and stays with me until I go on.

As I stood backstage on opening night, my blond wig was already itchy, hot, and sweaty. And I had to pee. Badly. But it was too late. (Story of my life— having to pee when it's too late to go is my body's code for: you're nervous and you might mess up!) Scottie Dog signaled me, and I walked out to the micro-phone. I looked through the sheet at the crowd at KeyArena in downtown Seattle. Over 16,000 people were staring back at me (or at my plain white bed sheet, anyway), waiting for me to perform. I felt really little up there onstage. I *was* really little! Why should *I* be up there? How could I ever win over

* It's my show and my ritual. You'd think I'd know why we say "pop off." But I don't.

105

that many people? But cheerleading had taught me to channel my fear into energy. I may have felt little, but I was ready to do everything bigger and better to compensate.

I took a deep breath, the sheet dropped, and I opened with "I Got Nerve." I didn't know if I could keep a crowd of 16,000 from throwing tomatoes at me (or maybe peanut-butter-and-jelly sandwiches—it was a young crowd). But I did know that I loved to sing, so I started by just focusing on that.

As soon as I started singing, I relaxed a little. After a while I felt calm enough to take a tiny peek at the audience. So I looked out . . . and I could not believe what I saw. It was a sea of Hannah Montana T-shirts! This audience wasn't there just for The Cheetah Girls. They knew who I was! (Or they knew who my TV character was when she wasn't herself. But let's not be picky.) When I started singing "I've Got Nerve," the crowd actually sang along with me. They knew every single word! Soon I could hear them chanting "Hannah!" and "Miley!" (See? They did know who I was. Or, rather, they knew who my TV character was when she was herself. But again, let's not be picky.)

My mom was backstage with my manager, Jason. They looked at each other and their mouths just dropped open. *What? This was out of control!*

So little time had passed since I'd been in sixth grade, holding back tears on a daily basis.* Those girls had made me feel completely worthless, invisible. But this was it: the equal and opposite reaction I had been hoping for. Here it was, proof that they hadn't stopped me. If anything, they had pushed me forward. For all that darkness, it wasn't over. Now a light was shining on me. **I was lifted up, not so much by success or fame or anything to do with Hollywood status as by the moment. My heart was flying. My soul was soaring. I felt radiant.**

Sure, if I could do it over again, I'd rather not suffer through those sixth-grade moments. But now, now that it was over, somewhere in the cruelty of those girls there was a gift for me. I'd put all the memories at the bottom of the ocean, but now that past floated back to me like a message in a bottle. I looked at it, felt happy, respected it, then threw it back again.

* my lowest low.

As I hit the final chords of "I've Got Nerve," I thought, "This is for them."

> *Even the hard times are part of your life story. If you acknowledge them and move past them, they eventually add up to the experience that makes you wise.*

I didn't stop to question what the audience's response meant about the show's popularity or my career. I recognized what was happening from my dad's concerts. Kids were singing along with every word. Parents were dancing with their kids. I looked at their faces and I saw joy. My dad always says that at that moment—when you, the band, the audience, when you all make music together—you become one. *That's harmony.* And that is what it is all for.

Life can be unpredictable and hard. There are plenty of bleak things in the world that we all could be thinking about. Maybe we should be. But on that night, in that moment, all singing along with each other? That was something we all shared, and while we were singing, whatever problems there were in the world, whatever troubles people were having at home, whatever bullies were waiting after school for some other kids in the crowd, to me it felt like maybe we'd put that all out of our minds for a tiny bit of time and just enjoyed one another's company. I brought the audience a little light. I had found a way to make people happy. That's as good as it gets.

I played twenty shows for The Cheetah Girls in one month, finishing on October 14 in Charlotte, North Carolina. Ten days later the *Hannah Montana* sound track—all music from the TV show—was released. My life was starting to feel like the best Christmas ever— each present was a new opportunity or news of a success I'd only imagined in my wildest dreams. The sound track debuted at the top of the Billboard charts.

Heck, yeah! Hannah Montana was no longer an opening act. She was a headliner. My dreams had come true. I was a singer. And an actor. So what if the dream come true had a straight blond wig glued on top? This girl wasn't complaining. You know that old expression: *A wig on the head is better than a head in the sixth-grade toilet.* Okay, maybe it's not the most common expression. Let's just say I know not to look a gift horse in the mouth!

Bad Luck in
St. Louis

Before we went on The Cheetah Girls tour, my mom made one demand. Usually when you're on tour for a concert, the whole crew stays on buses together. I was sharing a crew with The Cheetah Girls, so the total group was big—about a hundred people divided among maybe four buses. The dancers, two boys and two girls, were all in their twenties. I was thirteen years old. Mom said she didn't care if I didn't make a dime on the tour. She just wanted to make things as normal as possible for me. So we paid for an extra bus for just me, Mom, Mammie, and Noah. (The rest of the kids stayed in school.) After the show I'd come back to the bus, do schoolwork, then watch a movie with Mom and Noah. It was all weirdly normal. If there's such thing as normal when you're a teenager doing a twenty-city concert tour.

I was psyched that my mom went for the bonus bus. Being with the crew is fun for a little while, but it's impossible for me to live like that. I have to have space. I need the downtime. And it was more than just mental. Like I said before, weird or not, I'm okay being alone.

Even though the tour bus situation was sorted out, not everything was perfectly smooth on that tour. To be specific—two words represent how NOT smooth things were . . . St. Louis. I have nothing against St. Louis in principle, but I can't say I want to go back.

My bad luck in St. Louis started on that tour, and hasn't let up since. I was onstage in the middle of singing "Who Said" when I started feeling really sick, like I was going to throw up. I ran off the stage. It was really bad. My dancers just kept going. They didn't even notice I was gone!*

* Thanks, guys!

As soon as I started to feel better—about five minutes later—I hurried back onstage. I said, "Sorry, guys. I had to hurl." (Later my mom was like, "Real

\\\

classy, Miles. Guess you're never having dinner at Buckingham Palace.") Then it happened again. I had to run offstage during "Best of Both Worlds." So much for "the show must go on." I thought it was a stomach bug, and by the next day (we were still in St. Louis) I was feeling better, so I went on that night.

It happened yet again. Somehow I made it through the show this time, but in the next city, Dallas, I went to a doctor. He said I was fine, but at the show that night I felt bad again. This wasn't normal. And it wasn't nerves. Nerves meant having to pee when it was too late to go. This was different. Something felt really wrong. I went to another doctor, and this time they did an echocardiogram.* They found a hole in my heart (and this was *before* my first breakup!), but they said the real problem was tachycardia.

Tachycardia means my heart rate speeds up and the rest of my body can't keep up. (*Tachy* means too fast and *cardia* means heart. When I told Brazz my diagnosis, he said, "You sure it's not tachymouthia?") It just figures that if I had a problem, it would be that part of my body works harder than it should and goes too fast. I've always been an overachiever.

*An echocardiogram uses ultrasound to look at your heart. It's totally painless. Like when they look at a pregnant woman's baby except if they see a baby in your heart you're in big trouble.

The type of tachycardia I have isn't dangerous. It won't hurt me, but it does bother me. My heart rate increases a lot just from going up a flight of stairs. It's worse when I wear a wig. I get hot, my body tries to cool down, and my heart goes extra fast. When I wear that wig in a concert, it sometimes gets so I can't breathe and can't think. I feel claustrophobic. There is never a time onstage when I'm not thinking about my heart.

Psalm 43: 5

WHY AM I DISCOURAGED?
WHY IS MY HEART SO SAD?
I WILL PUT MY HOPE IN GOD!

My diagnosis stopped me in my tracks. On that tour, I felt like it was really important to me to look great. I wasn't eating much. Some days I'd eat one Pop-Tart. That was it. Not good. I've always struggled with my weight, but when I found out I had a hole in my heart—there was no way in heck being skinny was worth sacrificing my health. I was scared. Like lots of girls my age, I can be self-conscious about my looks, but it was immediately clear to me that I'd much rather be healthy and normal-sized. The minute I got home from that tour, my dad took me to one of my favorite Chinese restaurants, Panda Express. He said, "You have a hole in your heart, child. We're eating food."

I always thought that working as hard as I possibly could was the path toward achieving my dreams. But my body has limits that I have to respect. I have to take care of myself, or I'll feel sick. Now I make sure to eat well, get enough sleep, and avoid caffeine before shows. (That one was the only *really* hard one—I love Coke!)

On that tour, I learned that I can push too hard. It's easy to do. The fans would cheer me on, and the producers would cheer me on, and my family and friends would cheer me on. **But I'm the one in the driver's seat, and if anyone applies the brakes, it's got to be me.** It was an important lesson for me to learn. In a way, I think it's a kind of blessing that I have to be careful, because I should be taking care of myself anyway. It forces me to keep things in balance.

Yeah, and about St. Louis. The next time I went there—to sing the national anthem at a Cardinals game—the game got rained out. *And* St. Louis was the venue for the first show of my tour with the Jonas Brothers, which you would think was a good thing . . . but more on that later.

A "Normal" Day

After the tour with The Cheetah Girls, it was back home, and back to work on the set of *Hannah Montana*. That first morning home, I woke up at our house in Los Angeles to the voice of our alarm system saying, "Entry door open." That meant someone in my family was up walking the dogs. I dragged myself out of bed, brushed my teeth, showered, then opened one of my two closets.* Both are stuffed with more clothes than I could wear in a year. Half of the stuff is clothes I bought at Forever 21 and Walmart, and half is gifts from designers like Chanel, Gucci, and Prada that I began to get as the show took off. It's a quick glimpse of the two sides of my life—what I pick and choose and what people want to see me wear—all

* You read right—two closets!!

116

smushed together and tough to sort out in those closets.

As soon as I was dressed, I wrangled one of the legal-to-drive members of the household into taking me to the *Hannah Montana* set in time for 8 a.m. rehearsal. We broke for lunch at 12:30. My costars Emily, Mitchel, and I caught up, spilling out the lowdown on our lives in record time, then got back to work.

After rehearsal, I headed to a photo shoot for a cover of *Seventeen*, then went home to work on a song that needed to be ready for the next week's recording session. I had dinner with my family—except Dad, who was out of town, and Brandi, who was at her apartment—then went to my room to check e-mail.

I signed on to AOL and saw a candid shot of myself as the home page—not bad this time! Then I logged on to Miley World to read my fan mail. Then it was to bed, sleep, rinse, and get ready to repeat.

Yes, I too have a password to the Miley World Web site.

It was the second season of *Hannah Montana*. It was safe to say—my life had changed.

The Rest of Us

My new life didn't affect just me. It affected my siblings, too. But they are troupers. My little brother, Braison, is two years younger than I am. He's the sensitive one—he's very careful with other people's feelings. Brazz will come to me with anything, and we do our secret handshake over the most serious secrets. I'm not going to lie—I'm usually not good at keeping secrets. But when Brazz trusts me with something, nothing could make me break that trust. Someone could put a knife to me and I would not tell. Brazz and I became closer friends about a year ago. I don't want to pin it all on fashion, but I think it was when he got a pair of Converse sneakers. I was like, okay, you're not a wannabe preppy kid anymore.

Noah's the baby of the family and the comedian. She's a tough little cookie, and nothing gets past her. When Noah was four years old, a friend and I asked if we could do her makeup, and proceeded to paint her like a clown. We gave her bright pink circles on her cheeks and outlined a huge blue mouth. To this day she won't let me forget it. If I ever ask to put makeup on her, she says, "You're gonna make me look like a clown!" and refuses.

Noah wants her room to be like Noah's Ark. She's got a huge stuffed giraffe in one corner and a huge stuffed horse in another. She has fish, birds, and a dog. Noah wants as many animals around her as possible. That's what she and I (and our mom) have most in common. Nobody loves animals as much as we do.

Last year my mom and dad and Brandi went to a concert, and I stayed home to babysit Noah. As soon as they left, Noah said, "You're the fun one. I want to do something really fun." Who was I to argue? So I got out a big bowl and dumped in maple syrup, Coke, ice cream, whipped cream, some waffles, and sprinkles on the top. I gave Noah a spoon and said, "Let's see how much sugar we can get into you." She ate until she felt like she was going to throw up.

Then, to give her digestive tract a little time to recover, I decided to indulge her senses with a gentle and soothing spa treatment. I concocted a special custom facial for her out of eggs, honey, bananas, and . . . pretty much anything else I could think of. When my parents walked in the door, my mom said, "What's that smell?" The kitchen was a mess. There was food everywhere. And Mom was right, it didn't smell quite right. But in the morning, the first thing Noah did was put her hands to her cheeks and say, "My pores are so clean! My skin is baby soft." I was like, "That's because you *are* a baby." I am so glad I still get to experience moments like those. I would hate to miss them.

My older siblings are out of the house now, but they're still around a lot, and when they are I drop everything (except school and work) to spend time with them. Brandi is the angel of the family. She's the most honest and trustworthy person you'll ever meet. I mean, she's edgy—but she's also a really good girl. Trace is the carefree one. He doesn't worry what anybody thinks of him. Trace is super rock 'n' roll—I love his band, Metro Station. If I had to categorize our family, I'd say he's the one who's the most like me. Or, I guess I'm most like him, since he's the older one.

Now that I'm so busy I'm *very* aware of exactly how much time I have with my family. I want to make sure I make the most of it. It's not like we sat down and made rules like "Everyone has to be home for Tuesday pot roast dinner" or "Nobody talks on their cell phones in the living room." **Our house is a loud, busy place with family and friends and animals coming and going.** But, just like most people, we try to keep the stress—and definitely the work—out of the house. At home, I'm not a celebrity. Everyone still knows my name, but instead of chanting it at a show, they're shouting up the stairs for me to get my dirty laundry. At home, I'm just someone who has a job sooner than most kids do. The nice thing about our family is that everything I'm doing now is all stuff my dad has done for so long that when I started doing it, nobody paid much attention.

Homebodies

My dad has to travel for work, but when it comes down to it, both my parents are homebodies. Maybe that's why they get along so well. When my dad was touring with his mega-hit song, "Achy Breaky Heart," my mom stayed home with the kids. Dad was gone a lot, but even when he was home for as long as six months, my parents never went out on group dinner dates or had parties; they never entertained celebrities or schmoozed. They liked to be with each other and us.

I'm pretty much the same way. I like going to small parties and over to friends' houses, like ten people hanging out, maybe going for a swim. I'm always careful because of my heart. I guess my idea of a good party is someone getting their face smashed in a cake—not getting smashed. I don't drink and I would *never* smoke. I always say that for me, smoking would be like smashing my guitar and expecting it to play. I'd never do that to my voice, not to mention the rest of my body. My mom wants us to be careful not just about smoking, but about second-hand smoke too. What Mom doesn't? Both of my granddads died of lung cancer (even though Pappy's cancer came from asbestos, not from smoking), so I get why Mom is extra worried.

Too bad we get invited to lots of cool parties, because it's kind of wasted on us. After the Oscars last year, we were supposed to go to Elton John's party. We were invited to Madonna's party. There was some other dinner party that was a big deal. We had every ticket in town. It was dazzling and flattering. **But after the awards show was over, my mom and I looked at each other. I said, "I'll go if you want to go."** And she said to me, "I'll go if you want to go." There we were on Hollywood's biggest night, all dressed up, with every hot invitation we could imagine. So what did we do?

We stopped by our favorite local diner, Mo's, got barbecue chicken pizza, and went home to change into our pajamas. We were chowing down in the kitchen, talking about how much we like barbecue chicken pizza, when we paused for a moment and I said, "Should we have gone?" Then we shook our heads: *Nah*. When it comes down to it, we'd rather be home in our jammies.

7 foods I love

1. oatmeal with ice cream
2. grilled cheese with ketchup
3. macaroni and ketchup
4. potstickers
5. dumplings from Cracker Barrel
6. enchiladas
7. eggs with syrup

It's easy to be the same family we've always been when we're hanging out at home. But it's a little harder when we're out and about. Then the fame thing gets in the way. We like to go to church on Sunday and then to lunch together afterward. People will sometimes come up to us while we're eating. That's when my mom will say, "It's Sunday. We're eating. She's only sixteen years old, and she's not allowed to do that right now." I get embarrassed. Why can't I just do one signature? It takes five seconds. It's no big deal. But my mom says it's family time, and signing autographs can wait. She wants to make sure there are times when I'm just Miley, hanging out with my family.

Another thing that happens is that sometimes we'll go to Universal (the amusement park), and fans will gather, wanting to take a picture or to get an auto-graph. I don't mind doing it, but my family doesn't want to stand around for an hour waiting for me. They want to ride the rides. And suddenly I'm the sister who's slowing us down, and they're as annoyed as you'd be if your brother had a tantrum in the parking lot of a movie theater. Those moments, they remind me I'm still just Miley and I'd better get a move on.

Miles per Hour

When *Hannah Montana* proved a hit, life sped up for me and my whole family. It used to be that if I only had an hour to shop at the mall in Nashville or wherever, I felt rushed. How could I be expected to score the perfect jeans under such strict time constraints? Now I saw how much I could accomplish in just one hour. I could give an interview. I could write a song. I could learn calligraphy. I could get to level Hard in Guitar Hero. A free hour was now a huge amount of time to myself. It was a luxury. **You start to respect time a lot more when people constantly want to take it from you and you've got to decide what to do with it.**

On the other hand, I really hate how aware of the

I'm stuck at Hard. I'm not even that great at Hard, and I play Guitar Hero for at least twenty minutes every day.

passage of time I am now. I try not to feel like I'm on a clock. I like taking my time. If I'm getting dressed for the day, I want to make sure I'm comfortable. And I'm striving for a pretty high level of comfort. I might have to try on several different pairs of sweats before I settle on just the right ones. My mom's mellow too, but ever since our life became full of all these commitments, she likes to get to them on time. When she starts saying, "You're late, and you're making me late. I'm going to hit traffic," I say, "So what? Don't take me. We won't go. Or I'll just find someone else to drive me." I don't see any point in freaking out. I can't go into the past, reverse time, and make us *un*late. If we're late, we're late. Yeah, um, my mom still doesn't see it that way.

Go figure.

There are only so many hours in the day that I'm not on set taping the show. I do what I can to relax. I play Guitar Hero (which, I've almost convinced my parents, kinda counts as working if you're a professional musician. That's what I keep saying to them, anyway: "I'm a *professional* musician. I *need* this video game.") I kick back with my castmates during lunch break. Back in Tennessee, I used to make plans with friends after school (on days when I wasn't cheerleading). Now I do my best to keep the after-work hours free so I can go home and hang with my brother and little sister, riding bikes around the neighborhood or just being home. Things I can do without making an appointment or watching a clock.

So much of our lives is scheduled. It's go go go go . . . no! We have to say no sometimes. That can be hard for me—to figure out what to say no to. Everything sounds important. Everything sounds fun. But my parents are both really into reminding me that I don't have to maximize Every. Single. Opportunity that ever arises. My dad is the poetic one. He tells me to be real. To follow my destiny. And to remember that coming down the mountain is harder than climbing it. My mom is the practical one. The one who wants to make sure I have a childhood. The one who makes sure I help out around the house and save time for just hanging out with friends. I can't imagine what it would be like to have parents who thought I should push higher and higher for money or fame or popularity. That would definitely mess up my head.

The simple truth is that being at the top—the most famous or richest or most successful—isn't my goal. I don't have to be at the top. I don't want to be in the fast lane constantly. I realize I'm blessed to have had lots of experiences very few sixteen-year-olds get to have. But I also get that if I'm not careful, I might miss out on all the experiences every normal sixteen-year-old has. And with all the craziness, normal sixteen-year-old stuff is something I crave.

I know! Who wants normal teen angst??

Ecclesiastes 4:6

BETTER TO HAVE ONE HANDFUL WITH QUIETNESS
THAN TWO HANDFULS WITH HARD WORK
AND CHASING THE WIND.

When it comes down to it, my family makes it pretty darn easy for me to stay grounded and remember where I come from and who I really am.

My mammie comes to work with me every single day. She is the most amazing woman in the world. I've never heard her curse. I've never seen her mad. She lives every day counting her blessings. If I could, I'd make Mammie a saint. She's my second mother, and she is always there to keep my feet on the ground even when my head is in the clouds.

I know it is hard to believe, but we really are all about family and traditions. No matter how busy we are or what the day has in store, my dad loves to make me Ovaltine in the morning. He's been doing it ever since I was little, and he's a real perfectionist about it.

First he scoops the powder into a tall glass. Then he pours the milk. He stirs it all up, then gives it a slow, careful slurp. If it's not the exact right proportion of powder to milk, he'll say, "Nope, that's not quite right." I'm sure it tastes fine, and I try to stop him, but he says, "No, no, I want to get it right." Then he dumps the glass of chocolate milk down the drain and starts all over again. When he's finally got a glass that meets his strict standards of excellence (or maybe it's just an excuse for him to keep taking tastes for himself), we sit side-by-side at the counter and he drinks his coffee and I drink my Ovaltine, same as we have since I was little. It's still so satisfying. I look forward to it. I feel very lucky to have a dad who still thinks that chocolate milk is what I want to drink every morning. Do I actually *want* to drink chocolate milk every morning? It doesn't matter. Dad thinks I do, and, because of that, I do.

Drinking Ovaltine in the morning, making your sister look like a clown, eating late-night barbecue chicken pizza in jammies. It's the little things that make us who we are in the bigger world.

Southern Girl

Who I am has a lot to do with my family and where and how I grew up. Sure I was living my dream, but that hadn't happened overnight. So, where did that dream start? Partly on the stages where I watched my daddy perform. But mostly on our farm in Franklin, Tennessee, with a bunch of horses, cows, chickens, and my family.

People think that a farm is a lot of work, but if you're not, like, harvesting crops, it's not too hard to take care of animals. Horses can live in the wild, so you don't always have to do a lot for them. We put them out to pasture in one meadow, the cows in another. They eat the grass. The grass grows back. They eat more grass. Sometimes we ride them (the horses—not the cows); they're cool with it, and besides that, we just let them do their thing.

As for chickens, you can kind of make them into pets. My chicken, Lucy, will sit in your lap and let you pet her for hours on end. But you gotta start when they're little, or they turn mean. Lucy's our only sweet chicken. You're going to begin thinking I'm really back-country when I tell you this, but chickens are pretty darn fun to watch. They walk around bobbing their wonky heads. Seriously, there's nothing more relaxing than to kick back and watch chickens be chickens.

My mom always says that before I started school, our lives and schedules were based on an entertainer's schedule. My dad was on the road a lot, playing shows, coming home late. He often didn't get home until ten or eleven, so they'd let me stay up till all hours of the night, and then we'd all sleep late. Our time together was almost sacred.

Like I already said, when my dad was home I was his little shadow. I was four, maybe five years old when he'd saddle me up on a slow walking horse and take me, Braison, and Brandi out on the trails around our house.

(Trace was absolutely scared of horses and didn't like to go.) Or he'd sit me in front of him, and we'd go four-wheeling or dirt biking all day, ending up at the top of a hill where there's a tipi to camp in. (There's even a real totem pole that Pappy gave Dad!) Then Dad would build a fire and we'd roast marshmallows. **We'd sit there next to that fire, with the trees and the big Tennessee sky. It was easy to start dreaming big under all those stars. I felt like the sky was never-ending, like I could see Pluto. I spent most of my childhood outside with my dad.**

SOUTHERN GIRL

I remember ridin' horses
Playin' on a tire swing
Havin' little picnics watchin'
Leaves fall off the tree.

I love pickin' flowers
Puttin' my feet in the creek
Listenin' to the birds sing
While playin' hide-and-go-seek

These all might sound like li'l things
But they mean a lot to me

In the country there ain't much
But much ain't what I need
I'm a Southern girl
Big things don't really matter to me

I don't care what y'all see
Out in the big city
I don't know your so-called music
Just give me country.

As we got older, we still spent tons of time hanging out on the farm. Even when I was suffering through sixth grade, I'd come home and play a game of basketball with Braison or spend hours on the trampoline with Brandi. Out on the trampoline, we'd talk and laugh about . . . who knows? Nothing that made sense. That's the best part about hanging with a sister. You're not having conversations with beginnings, middles, and ends. You're just letting unformed thoughts bounce up and down and around and around.

At some point Trazz started building a treehouse between two beautiful trees. It was a work-in-progress for quite a while. Dad got into finishing it, but then he bashed his finger with a hammer and quit. Once I decided to help out. But since I have no clue how to build things, I just draped some blankets around what they'd built to make walls and a ceiling. You know, like a little kid's fort. But I kinda forgot to consider the rain factor. Yeah. Rain. Not so good when your little house has walls made from quilts. Still, the treehouse is very sweet as is. Whenever we go back to Nashville, Brazz and I like to sit up in the trees and play checkers. Our own little hideaway, where dreams can grow as big as we want.

Our family has never been really competitive. We always let each other win when we have games of chicken in the pool. We're careful of one another's feelings.

Too bad that caution with feelings didn't exactly translate into caution with vehicles. Let the record show that not one picture of me on a horse or a four-wheeler has me wearing a helmet. Dad always says he could've given some of those celebrity moms a run for their money in the unsafe parenting department. It never occurred to him to put us kids in helmets. Or to wear one himself, for that matter.

He has gotten better!

One time, when I was pretty young, Dad went four-wheeling with me in a papoose that he wore like a backpack.* Again, no helmets. He was flying through the woods, going pretty fast, zig-zagging along when he came to a tree that had fallen across the path. He ducked under it, but only as he ducked did he remember that I was on his back. *Whack!* He brought me home with a huge knot on my forehead. I can only imagine what I might have achieved if Dad hadn't given me minor brain damage. I'm still trying to come up with creative ways for him to make it up to me. Most of them start with the letters *C-A-R*.

* Don't try this at home!

Mule Day

I was talking about where the dream started, but before I go further, I have to digress and tell you about Mule Day. That's right, Mule Day. Pappy took me to it every year. Now, I'm not claiming that Mule Day played a huge role in making me want to be an actor and a singer, but I'm a girl from a farm and . . . come on, there's an annual celebration called Mule Day! It's part of my heritage. Don't you want to know about it? Hold on. . . .

I just called my dad and asked, "Am I dreaming, or did Pappy used to take me to Mule Day? What was it?" Dad said, "I would describe it as when every jacka__ comes to Columbia, Tennessee." So there you have it. I'm not making this up. (Don't they always say truth is stranger than fiction?) If you haven't been so lucky as to attend Mule Day yourself, it's an annual celebration of mules (and donkeys) held in Columbia. It features live music, arts and crafts, clogging, and, of course, mules galore. There's a mule sale, mule pulling, mule shows, and lots and lots of mule souvenirs. Pappy and I would come home with little miniature mules and mule T-shirts.

One day, to commemorate our mutual dedication to Mule Day, Pappy brought me a real, live donkey. He drove it all the way down from Kentucky in a horse trailer. He told me the donkey—I named him Eeyore—was half zebra, and that was why it had stripes on its ankles. It was only recently that I had my "Hey! Wait a minute . . ." moment and realized that *all* donkeys have white ankles.

So . . . Mule Day. Thought you should know about that.

My Little Breaks

There I was in Tennessee, watching chickens, celebrating mules, and risking serious injury at the hands of my four-wheelin' dad. I didn't have my heart set on being a huge star. Who does? But even then I knew I definitely wanted to perform in some capacity at least. A couple of years before we moved to Toronto, I went to "Kids on Stage," a summer acting camp at a little theater called the Boiler Room in Franklin. When our camp put on plays in the Boiler Room, I was never the lead. The only part I remember playing is an old woman. I think there was a wig involved, so I guess I did get *some* experience that would prove critical in later years.

At school I was way into doing plays, "way into"

being sort of the nice way of saying I was Miss Bossy. When my mom came in with me and my homemade costume, my second grade teacher, Miss Severe (also Brandi's teacher. And Braison's. And Noah's) said, "Miley has it all planned out." I was *that* kid. The teachers loved me.* Except when I wouldn't stop talking. Which was most of the time.

* The kids: not so much.

In fifth grade—one year before the infamous Year of Being Bullied—we finally moved to Toronto to be with my dad. My mom had been holding out, not wanting to uproot us from Tennessee, but like I said, we all just needed to be together. Leaving my cheerleading squad was the toughest change for me—I had been so into it. So my mom tried really hard to find a way for me to cheer in Toronto. Yeah—turns out cheerleading's not so popular in Toronto.

Mom finally found a squad in Burlington, an hour outside of Toronto. You were supposed to be in seventh grade to join, so I was too young; but she told them I'd been cheering since I was six and begged them to at least meet me. When I went out to the gym, they loved how teeny tiny I was. It was really easy to throw me all over the place. I got in!

Toronto was pretty darn cold compared to Nashville during a normal winter. The winter we decided to spend in Toronto turned out to be the coldest they'd had in fifteen years. So every Sunday we'd drive through a blizzard to Burlington for practice. My poor Southern mom, who'd never driven on an icy road in her life! She was a total hero.

In Canada, when I wasn't cheering or being home-schooled, I was always tagging along with my mom. That meant dropping by the set of *Doc* to see my dad. Being around the set so much, I absorbed a little bit about filming; how the camera blocking worked, what it meant when they said "Cut"; how important it was to be quiet. But mostly I liked trying on wigs in the wardrobe room. I know, I know. Some people look back on their lives and discover the theme to their life has been overcoming adversity, or battling injustice, or comforting the afflicted. So far, when I look back on my life, the only theme that I see starting to emerge is wigs.

My dad had been on *Doc* for a couple of years, and the producers all knew our family. Shortly after we arrived on the scene, the producer (or was it the director?) of *Doc* offered me the part of a girl named Kiley on an episode of the show. Kiley was an outgoing little girl with an alcoholic, abusive mother who came to live with her father in New York. Kiley's dad lived in the same apartment building as Doc (my dad). I had some good scenes as Kiley—some deep scenes dealing with the abusive mother, and a scene where Kiley tried out for the school play and got made fun of for her Tennessee accent. Little did I know how much I would need the experience. In two arenas: acting on TV *and* dealing with the mean girls.

If I had to pinpoint a moment, I'd say playing Kiley definitely gave me the acting bug. But mostly I have to mention it because it was nearly half of my professional acting résumé when I tried out for *Hannah Montana*.

After *Doc*, I started doing an actors' workshop and went to a few camps where I got to do monologues and plays. And I guess it paid off. The next time we were in Nashville on a visit to friends, my mom's friend Wendi* was taking her kids to audition for a Banquet Foods commercial starring country singer

* the one who later helped me write "I MISS You" about Pappy

143

Lee Ann Womack. I was curious, so she brought me along. Wendi's kids are younger than I am, so when the casting director said they were looking for an older girl for the spot, Wendi said I should go in. I don't remember what happened at the audition, but I got the commercial—and an agent in the process.

What I *do* remember is that the night before I went in to tape the ad, my mom cooked up some of the Banquet Foods products I'd be eating the next day. But when I came into the kitchen to have a taste, my brothers had eaten all of them. So they couldn't have been too bad—but I'm a picky eater. The next day, between takes, I ducked behind the table and spat out the beans (I think that's what they were) into my hand.

I guess nobody from Banquet Foods complained, because soon after that my new agent asked my parents to put me on tape for an upcoming movie directed by Tim Burton, called *Big Fish*.

Catching a Big Fish

Soon after the Banquet Foods commercial, we went back from Tennessee to Toronto, where we spent all our time trying desperately to stay warm. We lived on a lake. The lake was frozen solid almost all of that year. It was so windy that every time we took a walk I thought Baby Noah was about to blow away. We were freezing. But the idea of *Big Fish* definitely warmed me up.

Big Fish was big budget. It was a movie directed by Tim Burton starring Ewan McGregor, Jessica Lange, Albert Finney, Danny DeVito, and a ton of other well-known actors. The movie was being shot in Alabama. When we got the call that I'd gotten the part, they informed us I had to be there in two days.

YIKES!!

Mom didn't bat an eyelash. She said, "Alabama, here we come!" (Mom must have been pretty desperate to get someplace warm, because the minute she hung up she started throwing all of our clothes into the car.) Dad said, "You can't drive to Alabama! You're in Toronto!" But Mom was too busy fantasizing about sunny Alabama. Without pausing, she said, "Oh yes we can. We're crossing the border tonight."

Mom, Braison, Noah, me, and our nanny, A.J., left that night and drove fourteen hours straight to Nashville. How do you keep three kids under the age of twelve entertained on a more-than-twenty-hour trip? One answer: a DVD player. Mom was against DVD players until we started making those long trips up north and back. Even so, she should be given a Mother-of-the-Year Award for not ditching us on the side of the road.

As soon as we got into Nashville, Mom and I dropped A.J. and the other kids at home, dumped our Canada cold-weather clothes, grabbed some shorts and T-shirts, and kept on—straight down to Alabama.

The movie was being filmed in a teeny tiny town in the middle of nowhere. And coming from me, that's

saying a lot. We got to our hotel late at night and—
wow. It was the worst fleabag of a hotel in history.
There were cops roaming around outside—something
had just gone down—and inside, it was filthy. Mom
called Dad in a panic. He said, "Just get through
tonight. We'll work on it tomorrow."

The next morning we discovered the only upside to
the hotel from hell: it was connected to a Waffle
House. Mom and I like waffles. But not enough to stay.
We moved to a better hotel. Right after breakfast.

In the movie, I was playing a girl named Ruthie.
She was with a group of boys sneaking up to a witch's
house to look at the witch's eyeball. Ruthie was a
Goody Two-shoes Southern girl dressed in little Mary
Janes, telling the boys not to curse. Sounds pretty
straightforward, right? What Mom and I hadn't taken
into account was that the witch's house was in a
swamp. A cold swamp. A cold, wet swamp. A cold,
wet, *buggy* swamp. And it had been raining for weeks.
In our mad rush from Canada, we hadn't ever stopped
to check the weather. Let's just say we had not packed
for cold, or wet, or buggy. And definitely not for
swamp.

My call time was late because my scene was supposed to be taking place on a dark and spooky night. The first thing we saw when we got to our trailer were poster-sized pictures of snakes, spiders, and other critters that lived in the swamp. There was a sign that said WATCH OUT FOR THESE CREATURES! THEY'RE ALL VERY DANGEROUS AND THEY'RE ALL RIGHT HERE IN THE SWAMP, WAITING TO ATTACK ANYONE WHO CAME HERE FROM TORONTO AND ONLY BROUGHT SHORTS AND T-SHIRTS—WHAT WERE YOU FOOLS THINKING?! That's how I remember it, anyway. I was freaking out. Are you kidding me? Bugs? So sketchy! So scary! Bugs are *not* my thing.

Like I said, the swamp was wet and cold. There were weeds up to our waists. I was convinced the brown recluse spider on the poster was going to hunt us down and attack. Mom said, "Miley, are you sure you want to do this?" After driving all the way from Toronto? Heck, yeah, I was going to do it. Poor Mom. Our farm is one thing, but Mom isn't very outdoorsy. She was not having fun.

I wasn't exactly having the time of my life either, but I already knew that show business wasn't always a cakewalk. I remember watching my dad on the set of

Doc on a day when it was really cold out. People were getting frostbite. My dad's a big old guy, but it was so cold that he was tearing up. They had to get the shot. Not only that, my dad had to sit by a fountain looking like he was actually enjoying himself. I remember thinking, Dang, I don't know if I could do it.

Now here I was, on the set of a big movie. A little cold. A little wet. A lot nervous, with plenty of time to sit around and wait. They told us when we could eat, and they told us when we could go to the bathroom. It wasn't remotely glamorous. And that's the truth about show business. You see lots of glamorous moments in magazines, but most of it is plain hard work and little glamour. But you know what? I wouldn't trade it for anything! I had definitely gotten a bite—from the acting bug.*

Bugs or no bugs, I wanted to be really good in my scene. It was Tim Burton. If he liked me, he could put me in another movie. I was praying to do well, and concentrating really hard. In the beginning. But the later it got, the more unfocused I got. I just could not be quiet. When I start talking, there's no stopping

* Sorry! I couldn't resist that one!

149

me. I was even annoying myself. But luckily a movie set isn't the same as school. Me and my big mouth made it through without getting detention. As for that call from Tim Burton? I'm still waiting.

Back in Nashville, we went to see the movie when it came out. My whole family stood up and cheered when I came on the screen. I loved it. My mom got me the *Big Fish* poster, and I hung it in my room.

After that I got called back but rejected for the movie *The Adventures of Sharkboy and Lavagirl* (but at least I met Taylor Lautner at that audition—we've been friends ever since). Then I got called back but again rejected for the TV show *The Closer*. There was one audition—it was so painful I must have blocked what movie it was for. All I remember is that while I was auditioning for some movie starring Shirley MacLaine, one of my favorite actresses, the casting directors were making phone calls and completely ignoring me. I came out bawling. **When something like that happened my sister Brandi always told me, "Positive minds do positive things."** So I embraced that attitude and moved on.

My mom would see what I went through and say, "Honey, this is so hard. How can you take that rejection?" But they had raised me to be strong. I just came home and went back to cheerleading. I didn't think of it as failure. I thought of it as part of the route to success.

So you see I'm really not exaggerating when I say that when I started *Hannah Montana*, I'd done *Doc*, a commercial, and *Big Fish*. Period. Oh, and don't forget those old-woman parts with the wigs. No wonder Disney had their doubts about me. But I didn't. All those moments, from the farm to the swamp, had led me to now. I had dipped my toe in the water and knew I wanted to swim.

"Big Fish" . . .
swim. Get it?

Prince Charming

*H*annah Montana had only been on the air a few
months when I went to a benefit for the Elizabeth
Glaser Pediatric AIDS Foundation. I remember the
exact date: June 11, 2006. It was the day I met my first
love. Let's call him Prince Charming. I don't want to
use his name because this isn't about who he is or
what I meant to him. It's about how I felt and what our
relationship meant to me. Know what I mean?

So we were at this benefit, and I didn't know anything about the prince except I knew from a friend
that he thought I was pretty. He came up to me with a
bunch of guy friends and introduced himself.
Instantly, I wanted them all to go away and just to be
with him. He started to shake my hand and I said, "I

don't do handshakes. I do hugs." When he hugged me, I noticed his scratchy shirt and blurted out, "I hate your shirt." So that was just about the first thing I said to him: "I hate your shirt."

I had an insta-crush, so what did I do? Did I act smooth? Nope! I asked him to karaoke with me and put our names down for "I Want to Be Like You" from *The Jungle Book*. It would have been a funny, silly song to do together. But when the song came on I couldn't find him, so I had to karaoke all by myself. Let's just say people were laughing *at* me, not *with* me.

Later that night, he and his friends were going out, and he invited me along. My mom said she didn't want me to go out late—I guess I had a busy day the next day—so I asked her if I could just go for a little while. She said fine. So Brandi and I ended up going out to dinner with Prince Charming and his friends. I remember it took me forever to get dressed, but when I finally ran downstairs, I was wearing sweats. I didn't want look like I was trying too hard. Believe me, they were just the right sweats.

I liked him! I wanted to look cute!

After dinner we talked on the phone. He asked me

153

what my beliefs were. I said, "I'm a hard-core Christian." He said, "That's what we call ourselves in my family." I thought it was a sign.

We were on the phone that night until four in the morning. And, just like that, I was smitten. **It felt like the whole world stopped. Nothing else mattered.** I know it sounds silly, but my family doesn't set rules around love. My mammie met her husband on a Monday and they got married on Friday. They were together for twenty-seven years. My mom doesn't believe there's such a thing as being too young or too naïve to be in love. In my family, when you fall in love, that's it. No one called it puppy love or made fun of me. He really was my Prince Charming, and I knew it right away. You should have seen the sappy smile on my face when I hung up the phone that first night. I was mush. I slept holding the phone next to my cheek as if that would keep him close.

From the very beginning, we were best friends. We talked all the time. He lived on the East Coast but would fly to Los Angeles, and I'd see him when I was in New York. Then he moved to L. A., to a house—get this—a few blocks from mine, and everything got more intense and more fun. Suddenly we were neighbors. It felt natural and just so easy. He'd ask me to come over at five in the morning to say hi before I went to work, and I'd just walk down the street. In the beginning, when we were thirteen, we'd play basketball in my backyard or play Nintendo at his place. His family always made yummy Italian food for dinner. I love to ride my bike, and he'd walk along next to me as I rode, singing "My Girl."* But instead of "my girl," he'd say "Miley, talkin' 'bout Miley."

* by The Temptations

Wow! I was so in love. Do you know what I'm talking about? The kind of love where the sun could shine or not shine all day long and you wouldn't care. The kind of love that makes you want to jump in the pool in December. The kind of love that makes you want to dance in the rain. (Who am I kidding?—this is L.A. It never rains.) This was the most magical journey of my life—it was a total rush.

My Turn

You would think Prince Charming would distract me from my work, but it was actually kind of the opposite. I was in love, I had a lot to say about it—and good thing, because I needed to write a whole album of songs, pronto. The first *Hannah Montana* album came out right after The Cheetah Girls tour, and we immediately started planning the second. But this album was different. It wasn't just a sound track for the TV show. This album would have two discs—one with me performing songs from the show as Hannah Montana, and one called *Meet Miley Cyrus*, which would introduce me as a singer/songwriter in my own right. It was something totally new.

Wanting to sing wasn't new. I can't pinpoint a

specific moment when I discovered or decided that music was one of my callings, but the desire was always there. Sometimes it burned brighter. Winds and storms of emotion came and made it hot, scary. At times it felt dangerous to want something so much, and at times it was the easiest, most natural feeling in the world.

Dad always says that I could sing before I could talk. I'm a middle child, with kids older than me and kids younger than me. The older ones are responsible. The younger ones are adorable. Me, I'm in the middle, singing and dancing and generally making a big show of one kind or another in an endless effort to get attention. I'd put on my cowboy boots, Braison would put on his Reeboks, and we'd dance. Pretty much any time an adult came into our house, I'd drag them into a room to sing and dance and put on my show. If Mom and Dad had a guest disappear on them, they always knew to follow the sound of my voice. Wonder why I make YouTube videos with my friend Mandy? Boredom, salvation, laughs, and a middle child's endless craving for center stage. No matter how famous or successful I am, I'll always be an attention-craving middle child at heart.

My singing and acting isn't all about performance and getting attention, though. I've always had a strong response to art. When I hear a sad song, I don't feel sorry for the singer. I don't feel sympathy. Instead it's more like I take on the singer's sorrow. It becomes mine, part of who I am. If a sad song touches me right, I can be sad for weeks. I hear Bette Midler's "The Rose," and it's a song full of such sadness and hope that it fills me. Or some weird funk song says "I know lately you've been melancholy," and the word "melancholy" strikes a chord, hits my heart, speaks to me, and I can't help but respond. My little sister is the same way—she'll be affected forever if she listens to a sad song or sees a sad movie. We were born with that. Certain songs just change your life.

What that's grown into is the urge to do work that affects people. I'm not just talking about making sad music. It's not like I say to myself, *Hmm. I'm gonna write a song that makes everyone sad. That's just what the whole world needs right now—a little more darkness.* I mean something deeper. Creating art is all about

Sometimes being sad for weeks isn't ideal.

connecting. You look at a photo from the fifties, and suddenly you're connected to that time and place and spirit. You see a photo of a beach and summer memories flood back. Or you see a painting of Paris, and you're transported to the fantasy of a life you've never experienced. The reason I never want a book to end is that I start to feel like the characters are my friends. I'll miss them when they're gone.

Music (and other forms of art) does the same thing. It can inspire, lift you up to the future, rein in your pride, knock you off your feet, embrace your soul, change your life. I want to make that kind of music. Art is a gift to others. The purpose of art is to drown people in emotion.

> *If you can tune in to an emotion or experience that is universal, and draw it or sing it or write it so that other people recognize it and identify with it, then all those people you touched are brought together in their understanding, and the world is a smaller, friendlier place.*

Needless to say, I wanted *Meet Miley Cyrus* to be real—to achieve that connection with the people who were listening. We were starting to shoot the second season of *Hannah Montana*. It's always hard to find the right kind of time to write songs, but add filming a TV show to that. . . . An hour is a decent amount of time to work on a song I've already started, but for the most part I can only begin a new song when nothing's going on. So after dinner, on plane trips, whenever I could grab some time that felt unlimited, I took advantage of it to work on new songs. Then I went into the studio with some songs written and some that I was still trying to finish.

Prince Charming and I had been together for almost a year at this point, and things were mostly good. So lots of the songs on *Meet Miley Cyrus* were songs for and about him. I'd call him every night and say, "I wrote you another song!" People might wonder how I could write so many songs about one boy, but I knew I could write him a bajillion songs. Actually, now that I think about it, most of the songs on that album were about Prince Charming.

Don't get me wrong. The relationship wasn't perfect. But I think about it a lot like the farm, and how everything is so tranquil there. Yes, there are storms, but even the storms feel natural, like part of what is meant to be. I would always want to let the storms carry me away. On the other hand, sometimes you would rather have endless days of blue skies.

At some point we decided that we needed to take a break. I thought we were going to break up for good. I was so brokenhearted that I wrote "Girls' Night Out" to make myself smile. But immediately afterward I wrote "Right Here" to play for him as a way of telling him how much I loved him. To tell him: **No matter what, I'll be there for you. No matter where we are in life.** And then some of the songs on the album, like "Clear," are what I think of as "pre-breakup" songs, where I'm imagining what it would be like to break up and how much that would suck, and kind of taking on that emotion.

I went into the recording studio on weekends, squeezing time in whenever I could. I'd work on a song at home, then sit with it a little while to see how it felt, making changes here and there. Before I'd worn it out, I'd take it in and record. Sometimes for art to be really the best it can be, no matter how personal it is, you have to bring in other people to help. If I can trust one person in the world with my music, it's my producer, Antonina. She is my dream girl, my role model. When I come in with a story and pieces of a song, the two of us can work it into a real song, and I know she'll never tell anyone where it started, what it meant, and how it evolved. After I recorded my part, the rest of my producers worked on the songs, layering sound effects and instruments. I got versions along the way, hearing each song again and again until they were all how we wanted them.

After three or four months of visits to the studio, there it was—my first album as myself. Well, half of a double CD anyway. Hannah was still carrying me. It was Hannah who made so many copies of the album sell. But whenever I worried that all my success was due to Hannah I was like, wait a minute! I *am* Hannah! I worked hard to be that character and to make her my own. So Hannah wasn't carrying me. I was carrying both of us.

If that makes any sense at all!

7 artists I admire

1. Beethoven

2. Picasso

3. Stevie Wonder

4. Celine Dion

5. John Eldredge

6. Antonina Armato

7. Metro Station

O! Say Can You See

That spring, I was invited to perform the national anthem at the 2007 Easter Egg Roll—at the White House. The White House! I was definitely excited, but surprisingly, I wasn't nervous. The fear and anxiety that I once felt in auditions and in early performances —it was gone. I grew out of it. I think everyone does at some point. You realize you have one life—and you have to live fully for the moments you have. There can't be room for nerves.

My mother, my grandmother, my dancers, and I flew to Washington just for the event. It was cold for April, so I borrowed an outfit from one of my dancers, Jen (their outfits are just as blinged-out as mine). Laura Bush (that's right, folks, the former First Lady) introduced me. And then I sang on the same balcony where the president does his speeches. (Wouldn't it be cool if after every presidential address some singer appeared on the balcony and rocked out? You know— here's the State of the Union, and then there's me singing. Oh, just let me have my little fantasy!)

After I sang, I went downstairs where a bunch of kids, Clifford the Big Red Dog (or at least a person in the costume), and some other important political figures were milling about. I even did some back handsprings on the South Lawn.

Now that's something I'll want to tell my grandkids.

The Egg Roll was around the time I wrote "Girls' Night Out," meaning Prince Charming and I were on a break. We were young and living strange lives.

But it just so happens that he was also at the Egg Roll. **The instant I saw Prince Charming, my heart did a cartwheel.** (I was doing a lot of actual—and metaphoric—tumbling that day.) It didn't matter how we fought, what was said, how hard it might be, or if we were taking "time." There was no question in my heart. We were back together. Or we'd never broken up. The point was, everything was right in the world.

7 things I want to change about the world

1. end world hunger

2. homeless people without the comfort of a snuggly bed and family to go home to

3. mean online message boards

4. school bullies

5. not everyone having clean water

6. nasty hormone-infested chemical-laden inorganic food

7. bring PEACE ☮

I know that I've had some pretty remarkable moments in my life so far. But I'll *never* forget that day—singing at the White House, introducing Mammie to Laura Bush, and falling in love all over again.

About Face

* Well, I was
still stuck
on Hard,
but at
least I was
enjoying
myself.

So there I was. I had my dream job. I had great friends and family. My Guitar Hero scores* were getting better. Everything was ~~good~~.** And then, ** No suddenly, it wasn't.

One morning I couldn't get out of bed. It was near the end of the second season of *Hannah Montana*. There was a lot going on. The show had proven so successful that Hannah Montana had gone from being a character to being a brand. There was a tour coming up, the albums, press, endorsements, charity events, and lunch boxes. I wouldn't have been surprised to step into my bathroom and find Hannah Montana toilet paper. (Though I'm not sure exactly what I would have done with it.) It sounds exciting, and it was, but in a weird way I was removed from it all. Disney executives were making all the big decisions about Hannah. I just got told where I had to be and when I had to be there. On the set, after work, weekends, I was going full steam. It definitely took a toll on me.

I would like to say it was exhaustion or the pressure of new fame, but that's not why I couldn't get out of bed on that particular morning. The truth was, I couldn't get out of bed because my skin looked awful. **I didn't believe I was beautiful. Nothing could change that fact.**

My dad had had bad skin as a teenager, and mine had slowly gotten worse as the season went on. I'm sure all that stage makeup didn't help. And as if the mirror wasn't sending the message loud and clear, people on the Web started making comments.

Makeup. ✓
Stress. ✓
Lack of sleep. ✓
Fourteen years old. ✓
Being made fun of on the Internet. ✓

Beauty is the enemy. We try to conquer not feeling beautiful all our lives. It's a battle that can't be won. There's no definition of beauty. The only way to achieve beauty is to feel it from inside without breaking it down into individual physical attributes.

How could I show up at work? I couldn't let them film me looking like this. How could I go outside? I couldn't let a fan take a photo of me. I usually go to the gym in the morning. But how could I deal with all those mirrors?

I couldn't take it anymore. It wasn't just the zits. I honestly believed there was nothing special about me. I refused to get up. I couldn't move. Hours went by. Then it was two p.m., and I was supposed to be at the studio for work. My mom had been coming in to check on me, and by now she was threatening me, saying, "I'm going to call your dad. He's going to have to fly home." She wanted to get me out of my bedroom and back into the real world, out in the daylight. But it wasn't that simple.

If you ask me I don't
Think I can explain.
My heart knows the truth but
Hasn't told my brain.
Sometimes I wish I could fly away
'Cause I don't know how much longer I can stay.

Eventually my mom got me to go to work that day, but the darkness didn't go away. I'd see myself in makeup, or Photoshopped in magazines, and see this perfect, airbrushed version of myself. Then I'd look in the mirror and see reality. You know how all those magazines are doctored, how none of the models or celebrities or stars look as good in real life as they do when they've been dressed, styled, made up, and airbrushed? Well, if you ever find yourself wishing you looked as good as Miley Cyrus in some photo (and I'm not so vain as to assume you would), just remember: *Miley Cyrus* doesn't look as good as Miley Cyrus in that photo. Take it from me. I became obsessed with the way I looked. I'd stare at the mirror for hours, hating myself outside and in. If all eyes were on me, why did I have to look like this?

It started with my skin, and then it snowballed. I didn't like my looks, my body, my personality, anything about myself. Why would God do this to me? I know, I know, melodrama. A few zits don't exactly make me Job. But cut me some slack. I really am a teenager. On better days, I know that superficial things shouldn't matter. I know I'm supposed to put it in perspective. But that doesn't mean I'm good at it yet.

7 things I'd like to change about myself

1. how loud I am
2. my frizzy hair
3. my bad skin
4. my love for cupcakes
5. my toenails
6. my way to an honest self
7. my snorting laugh

We needed to at least try to fix my skin. So I went to a dermatologist. I had high hopes. I figured: this is Los Angeles. L.A. doctors had to have all sorts of magical ways to instantly make actors look perfect. I thought they'd, like, airbrush me in real life with special cover-up that would last until my twentieth birthday. Yeah, not so much.

If you've ever had acne, you know that there's no instant solution. I walked out of that office more depressed than when I went in. My mom tried to reason with me. She said, "Every day when you wake up you have a choice to make. You can decide to be mad at the world, or you can decide that this isn't going to affect you. You won't have this problem forever. We're working on it. But meanwhile you have to remember that there are a lot worse things in the world." I know Mom learned that way of living from Mammie. Mammie always says, "All things work together for the good." But this time I rolled my eyes. Of course there were worse things. Now I was ugly *and* self-obsessed. But Mom went on, "I know that doesn't make you feel better, but you do have a choice about how you're going to deal with things every day. You can be angry and upset. Or you can tell yourself that you have acne just like everyone else." I listened to the words she was saying, but they just floated around me. I couldn't—*wouldn't*—take them in.

The whole end of the season was a miserable, hard time for me. I wasn't talking to anyone on the set, I was surly, I was late. I didn't really talk about it to most people. For the most part, they had no idea how twisted up I was, though at some point the AD (assistant director) on the show was like, "Where's Miley? This isn't our Miley." He was right. It wasn't me. I don't usually hold on to thoughts that drag me down, but this time I couldn't let go.

When the AD came up to me and asked what the deal was, I told him about my skin (although that wasn't all of it), and he talked to me about his own struggles with acne. I looked around, and it occurred to me that everyone has a history of obstacles. I knew I wasn't the only teenager with acne, but I also got it that people live through it. **You deal. You survive. You grow up and you build a career. And you remember these big/little hardships. They make you human.** Talking to the AD, to my mom—none of it was the magic cure, but I slowly managed to keep getting out of bed. That was the best I could do.

When the season ended, I was busier than ever. I was about to go on tour and didn't have time to think. I was always dancing, sweating, out late working. The distraction helped. But when I went home, and the distractions were gone, the self-hatred would hit me all over again. I'd lost perspective.

The Luckiest Girl in the World

The loss of perspective wasn't just because of my skin. I was getting a lot of attention, even for a middle child like me. It was affecting me. I was self-absorbed and unhappy. I knew that there were bigger problems than mine, but I couldn't see beyond my own issues. I was being a brat. Stardom had changed me. I wasn't Miley anymore. I was Hollywood. Something *had* to shift.

Remember how I said that when I was growing up my dad went straight from his performances to donate the flowers and gifts he received to the closest children's hospital? Well, he did that all the time. I was raised visiting hospitals with my dad and with churches. When I started working on *Hannah Montana*, I made sure to keep doing the same. These kids didn't have much to smile or laugh about. They were powerless to change their situations. They were angry, with nobody to blame. They had no relief from their sicknesses and their frustrations. But many of them were fans of the show, and I came to see that when they were watching it, for that thirty minutes, they were distracted from their pain, maybe even happy.

When that second record, *Meet Miley Cyrus*, came out, I was still in a funk, still depressed and full of self-hatred. Then I went to a children's hospital to give everyone the new CD. Kids who hadn't smiled for a long while, smiled. One little girl pulling an oxygen monitor came in to meet me. She was going through yet another round of chemotherapy. She had no hair remaining, and little time left to live. When I handed her my CD, she said, "I'm the luckiest girl in the world." It was so hard to see. She was dying before my eyes.

Childhood cancer is impossible for me to understand. My pappy was a big, strong man, but cancer made him cry, and if my pappy cried, I know he was in more pain than any human should ever suffer. **To imagine a child enduring that . . . To get a disease when you should be playing ball and pretending to be a princess and jumping rope . . . A small child with no experience or wisdom to help them through it—I just can't bear it.**

If such a small gesture as a visit and a little music can make a child happy, then I sure want to do that kind of thing as often as humanly possible. When I visit, I don't like to leave until I've gotten them all laughing. When I can't visit in person, I make phone calls to kids in hospitals. When I can't call, I send videos. I'm not vain. I'm not, like, *Oh, I'm Miley Cyrus and I'm so special that I change kids' lives.* But if this career gives me any power, I want to use it right. So if I can make a day a little brighter, you better bet I'm going to do it.

Coming home from the hospital that day, I felt the darkness shift a little. I was so sad and moved and full of prayers for the children I had met. Seeing the children suffering—and surviving—was a jolt. How could I think about my skin problems—and all the other

7 things I wish were true

1. a cure for cancer is coming
2. the 80s style is back
3. everyone loves each other
4. I'm a good painter ☺
5. Johnny cash is alive
6. we can rewind time
7. the stars tell our future

self-criticism—when I had so much to be grateful for?

A few weeks later, I met Vanessa, a person who would change my life forever. It was before a Disney event at a hospital in Los Angeles. Vanessa was nine

* No, Disney
didn't pay
me to
write
this.

** Actually,
Disney did
pay me to
write this,
but they
didn't tell
me what
to say.

years old and had cystic fibrosis. The night I met her she was wearing a Cinderella costume.* But she looked just like Ariel from *The Little Mermaid*.** She had green eyes, dark skin with freckles, and glowing red hair. I said, "You look so beautiful," and she said, "You do too," and gave me a huge hug. There was something in that hug that touched me. She was angel-like. Something passed between us. I just knew we were meant to be friends. It was like my first meeting with Prince Charming. We were friends at first sight. We talked for a while longer, and when I had to go I asked my mom to get her mom's e-mail address so we could stay in touch.

That night after the Disney event, I had to go to the studio to work on a song. But when I got there, I couldn't do it. I felt tears threatening to spill over. I pretended to be sick to get out of the studio because I didn't want to cry in front of everyone. I just couldn't sing. Music is everything to me—I love being in the studio. But all I wanted was to hang out with Vanessa and make sure she was okay.

I was anxious to go back and see her again, but my mom couldn't find her mom's e-mail. Mom loses

She denies this.

everything. She loses her cell phone at least once every day. So we went back to the hospital without knowing how to find Vanessa. I didn't even know her last name. I didn't know anything—just that there was something special about Vanessa. Reception at the hospital couldn't help us; we had my dad on the phone at home looking through my mom's stuff. Finally the head of the hospital showed up and knew exactly who she was. He told us she'd gotten to go home for a week. So the next week we came back and surprised her. I'm a weird mix of mature for my age and immature for my age, and Vanessa was the same way. We had a special connection, and quickly became true friends.

I invited Vanessa to come visit me on the set. She was on oxygen and kept coughing. Her mom would pound her on the back to help the coughing stop. I was told that she might live to thirteen, she might live to twenty. She had to be very careful not to get sick. I had to wear a mask around her. And when she wanted to borrow her mother's lip gloss, her mother said she wasn't allowed to because of the germ factor. She started crying. "Everyone else gets to wear makeup," she said, and I knew that that was only the tip of the iceberg.

I had been praying to God to take away my vanity and self-centeredness. All I had to do was turn on the news or flash back to the suffering kids I'd met to realize how petty I was acting. **When I met Vanessa, all the superficial obsession over my skin, and all the darkness I'd been feeling, fell away.**

September 21, 2007

Today is the last day of Season 2 of <u>Hannah Montana</u>. Yes, this is the end of one journey, but it is just the beginning of this new path. I will never let my dreams die and I will remind myself of all my blessings as I write. I will continue to believe that I can do anything & Christ will be by my side every step of the way!

I will never forget all that I have been given. I will be leaving for my first headlining tour in about one month, where I will be surrounded by family and friends.

I am blessed! ♡

That was one of Vanessa's gifts to me—perspective. You can't suddenly gain perspective just because your mom tells you (nicely—over and over again, but still nicely) to snap out of it. You need to see things, *really* see them, feel them, live them, so you know what's big and what's little, what matters and what to put aside.

I'm not saying I don't still sometimes get caught up in that stuff. When I read online that people think I have "cankles" (which means calf-ankles), I kind of had a fit. My dad said, "That's okay, honey. All the Cyrus women have cankles. It's a family trait. You should be proud." Thanks, Dad. I never thought I had the tiniest ankles in the world. But now I had Internet confirmation that my fabulous cankles were obvious to one and all. I was so upset when I read the cankles comment that my mom confiscated my computer.

The biggest moments of insecurity come when all self-confidence is lost and you feel like people are watching and judging. It should be the opposite. You should feel like the people who are watching care about you. This is something we can try to give each other—the feeling that eyes signal support, not disdain.

I'm young. I have my moments. How can you always have perspective if you haven't lived for very long? I don't think it's possible. But you can try. I want to be a person who focuses on the positive. I'm living an incredible life, and I never forget to be grateful for that. I try to remind myself that with that life comes some challenges. People can be mean or spiteful or envious or resentful or judgmental. Or they honestly hate my ankles, and it's important to them to express that in a public forum! Whatever. It's part of the gig, and I wouldn't trade the gig for anything. That's what I tell myself (and Mom reminds me) when the meanness and pettiness get to me. Keeping things in perspective takes work, and, like everything I do, I try to give it 110 percent.

MILE THREE

Broken Up and
Breaking Out

Meet, Greet,
Sing, Sleep

October 14, 2007

Today is our first day of tour—we're in St. Louis, & the next 3 days are rehearsals and then we have our first show—being with my friends and the Jonas Brothers will be a blast! I am so excited to start and be doing what I ♡ with the people I ♡ ! Today we were on the coolest jet— we saw Daddy and had a blast!
♡M Miley

In a way, the whole idea of going on the Best of Both Worlds tour felt comfortable. After going on tour with my dad and The Cheetah Girls, I knew what it was like

media, all the time.

Radio Disney!

MTV STUDIOS

Flying in style
never gets old!

Skyward bound on my way to be on <u>oprah</u>!

Traveling in style to my concert in San Diego.

Family :)

Stretching
it
out.

At the <u>White House</u> with my best friends!

✕✕✕

In front of the Arc de Triomphe!

Brandi & I having our own rockin' New Years in Times Square!

TELEPHONE TELEPHON

My first trip to London. I'm such a tourist!

♡ my horse!

My 1st
coffee shop
concert!

My grandma Ruthie.
She's always there for me!

Thank you
4 the crew!

07/17

Getting warmed up before a big show—my choreography needs a little work.

Mommy & me

Always time for a little goofing off!

This part is always fun—walking underneath the stage before my opening number.

Scottie

Performing rocks!

XO!

Loving Life!

to have a bus as your home base, to wait backstage for the music to come up, and to hear a stadium full of people chanting. Except this time they wouldn't be chanting my dad's name, or Hannah's name for that matter—if I was lucky, they'd be chanting for me!

During my first tour, opening for The Cheetah Girls, I performed as Hannah the whole time. This time, not only did I have top billing, but I got to do half the show as myself. It may not seem all that different to the people in the audience—I mean, I use the same voice to sing the songs—but it feels *really* different to me.

Hannah has a different message. Hannah's songs are about what it's like to be a famous person when you're an ordinary girl at heart. Her songs, like "Just Like You" or "Best of Both Worlds," are fun to sing, but I am not as emotionally attached to them. I focus on the choreography and moving the way Hannah moves. In a way it's easier for me than being myself, but it's also hard for me to get into that character.*

* And to wear that wig!

Performing my own music is the coolest feeling in the world. My songs are about things that are meaningful to me. Missing a grandparent. Mistakes that I've made in relationships. Things that make me happy or disappoint me. I feel that as myself, I connect to my audience more.

And it was a *big* audience. Let me run through some numbers really fast. The Best of Both Worlds was my first headlining tour. It ran from the middle of October 2007 till the end of January 2008. I played 68 shows in 59 different cities. Each stadium seated between 10,000 and 20,000 people.

If I counted right.

You know how they tell performers to "break a leg?" Well, about a week into the tour, in Salt Lake City, I almost did. There was a move during "I Got Nerve" where four big, strong male dancers were supposed to throw me in the air and then, of course, catch me. But that night they popped me too hard, which meant I went higher and came down faster and with more force than planned. The dancers weren't ready for how hard I was coming. I went right through their arms and fell onto the stage. Of course, this was during the "Hannah Montana" part of the concert. The "Miley Cyrus" part of the concert didn't have any moves like that. It wasn't very me. The problem was, if Hannah Montana broke her leg, so did Miley Cyrus.

I was lucky. No broken leg—this time. I was up and dancing again in a split second, but not before I heard the audience gasp. Then a whisper went around the stadium as everyone turned to the person sitting next to her to say "She fell!" As I went on with the song, those words tugged at my mind.

> *Embarrassment is the worst! It's the feeling of having your entire body go numb and not knowing what to do with yourself for that one moment. There's no solution to embarrassment. It happens, and you just have to put it behind you.*

Falling like that is my worst nightmare. It didn't hurt, but it was embarrassing, and I hate that feeling more than anything. They re-choreographed the move to make it safer, but the next night I was terrified that they would drop me again. "Don't make me do it! Do I have to do it?" I pleaded with the director to cut the pop from the routine. But there was energy in that move that we wanted to give the audience.

My mom reminded me about cheerleading. She was right—in cheerleading you fall all the time, you fall so often that you practice getting good at falling, and then you fall some more. You never quit. I thought about my cheerleading coach, Chastity, and how she would have said, "Don't hit the ground." But I still dreaded being dropped, every single night. I remembered a coffee mug I saw once that had a Ralph Waldo Emerson quote on it. *Do what you are afraid to do.* And so I did. I kept going. I just did it. Now, when I think back on it, I realize that each day of the tour I achieved something, because every day I overcame my fear. The fear of being embarrassed can hold me back from doing things I want to do. I'm holding on to that memory as proof that fear doesn't have to win.

I performed almost every single night, which is draining, but the tour was also kind of easy just because it was the same routine every day.

10-ish: Wake up on the bus

12:30: Sound check

1:30: Hair and makeup

3:00–5:00: Meet and greets

5:30: Opening band starts

6:00: Concert starts

10:00: Back in bus

Every day revolved around the performance that night. The morning was spent doing sound check and getting ready, then I had "meet and greets" with friends of friends, people who won contests, whoever it was. I love my fans, but the meet and greets were different, mostly executives or other people who wanted something from me—like tickets to that night's show, which I never had. It's hard to be excited and friendly to strangers every single day. There was kissing up in all directions, and the whole thing felt like a show, a game with no rules, no winner, and no limits. Whatever time and energy I gave, someone always wanted more.

My parents were always there for me, of course. For the most part they don't want to take any of this away from me. This is my work, and they want me to have independence in it. But I can get too drawn into it, into feeling I need to satisfy every request, take every media opportunity, meet every fan, sign every deal. I found out later from my mom that she had decided I wouldn't do any press on the tour. Not a single newspaper interview, radio show, or TV appearance. I was a little angry—I mean, it's my career, and I like to be in on those decisions. But my mom knows that it would be hard for me to say no. There's no end to the requests and demands for my time. People will push until I can't take it anymore. I'm young, and people forget that. Including me. There's no way I can make everyone happy.

The days on tour were a whirlwind of obligations, and then I'd do my show, and then, late at night, (when I didn't fall asleep before my head hit the pillow), thoughts would turn endlessly in my mind. My brother Trace was in Europe. I didn't have time to visit him. Should I be visiting him? What about my sister? Should I be worried about her? Should I be thinking about the show? My fans? My family? Was I forgetting someone's birthday? Where was my energy supposed to go? Was I a good person for spending my time this way? There were lots of people working on my tour. There were tons of people coming to each concert. I was the center of it, and I didn't want to do it blindly, going through the motions because some producers or marketers thought it was a good idea, or because I was going to make money, or even because I like performing and wanted to introduce people to my music.

My dad says, "Not everyone was called to be a preacher. There are different ways of representing the light. If you can make people laugh and sing and dance and rejoice in this world of darkness, that's a great thing." It's important to ask yourself why you're doing what you're doing and what purpose it serves in the big picture. I ask myself that a lot.

On The Cheetah Girls tour I had performed for cancer patients. I'll never forget how it felt to know that kids who couldn't be happy on a daily basis were at my concert. I vowed to myself to make sure I always performed for the right people and the right reasons.

After I met Vanessa, one thing was clearer to me than ever before. I knew I wanted to actively help children who needed it. For the tour, I worked with Bob Cavallo and Hollywood Records, one of the companies Bob Cavallo oversees, to give one dollar of every concert ticket to City of Hope, a cancer care center. Making people laugh and sing and dance is an incredible feeling, but I also wanted to give something as big as hope to people like Vanessa. Whether the audience knew it or not, each one of them was (through me) giving a dollar to City of Hope. We were all united in an effort to help people suffering from cancer. When our family first moved to Los Angeles, our goal was to try to be light in a dark world. Now I was doing it. As I performed in concert after concert, I kept that in the back of my mind—the knowledge that what I did that night would go further than what everyone in the stadium saw or felt.

Despite all the positive things going on, being on the road can get lonely. We were never in one place for more than one night. My "home" was the tour bus. I slept on a built-in bed. Plenty of times I just wanted a break, to go home for real. But I was lucky to have my friends and family on tour with me. People were what got me through it. I tried to think of them as my home. Isn't that a saying, too? Home is where the heart is?

I know I talk a lot about my dreams. How can I not, when my life has taken such a dramatic, surprising, exciting turn for the most amazing? The tour was one big gigantic, elaborate, exhilarating, exhausting dream come true.* I should have known something had to go wrong. It's inevitable—dreams fade or change eventually.

*Except for that one hairy dance move.

No Such Thing as a Hate Song

Prince Charming and I broke up on December 19, 2007. The hardest day ever. My life felt like it had ground to a halt, but the rest of the world kept right on rolling. I was on tour. People were counting on me, but my head—no, my heart—was dizzy.

I've always used words to connect with people, and I've always felt that if I just let the words flow, just said what came to me, it would be from the heart and I would be understood. The day before the tour ended I wrote ten pages, front and back, about why I loved Prince Charming, how I would wait for him, why we needed to be together. When I love someone, I love them with everything in me. But when the love's not there anymore, what do you do?

Deep down I knew we weren't being our best selves. And that was what I wanted—and thought I deserved—in a relationship. To be my best self and to bring out the best in someone else.

But still . . .

I was angry when I wrote "7 Things I Hate about You." I wanted to punish him, to get him back for hurting me. It starts with a list of what I "hate," but I'm not a hater. My heart knew from the start that it was going to turn into a love song. Why does he get a love song? Because I don't hate him. I won't let myself hate anybody. That's not the way my heart works. It's a song about how I should hate him but I don't, and I don't know why. It's a song about forgiving, not forgetting.

you're vain, your games, you're insecure

There's a big difference between knowing and feeling. Here's what I know:* I know I'm "only six- teen." I know that most people when they're older look back on when they were sixteen and think, "Man, I didn't know anything back then." I know that what I want, what I look for in a boyfriend, is bound to change a lot, because I know I've got a lot of changes

So far.

7 things that make me sad

1. my pappy dying
2. that my parents will never know how much I love them
3. my horsies being in Nashville without me
4. people who don't know Jesus
5. kids with parents who don't kiss them goodnight & tell them how much they adore them
6. my brother being on tour without me
7. world hunger

ahead of me still. I know all that. I really do.

Here's what I feel: **It's hard to imagine that our love is a story with an end**. But you know, at least I'm getting some really good songs out of it.

Another Angel

October 31, 2007

It's 1:02 a.m. and I'm not able to sleep after the painful news received around eleven that my best friend, my hero, my sister God forgot to give me, my everything was graced with 24 hours to live. I don't know why this happens and why it will continue—all I know is I will have a new angel watching over me, and her name is Vanessa.

My friend Vanessa was very ill.* They were saying it was only a matter of hours. But I was in denial. When I called the hospital hoping to hear that she was on an upswing, because that's what I wanted to believe, her parents told me, "Miley, she died."

* Remember? The sick little girl who looked like Ariel?

I couldn't process it. She was dead? But she was so young. I couldn't accept it. How could she die? How could God feel like her job here was done? I'd never lost a friend before. I was wrecked.

It was late at night. We were stopped at a Walmart in the middle of nowhere. I couldn't get back on that bus. I needed things to halt. I went out into the middle of a snow-covered field and lay down. The sharp blades of frozen grass poked at my bare arms. I lay on my back staring at a big white sign saying SUPERMART. Vanessa was gone, and I hadn't been there by her side at the end.

After a while, Linda, my teacher, and my mom came out to get me. Linda said, "Look how happy you made her. She had a good last few months. When she needed you, you were there." My mom said, "You knew she needed you, but it seems like you didn't realize how much you needed her."

I CAN'T BREATHE

I can't tell you why the sun shines
I can't explain the moonrise
I don't know why time flies by
But ask me and I'll tell you why—
[Chorus]
I'm blessed to have you in my life
I can't live another day without you by my side
It's gettin' harder and harder to breathe
So I'm beggin' you
Don't take her away from me

I've known since I met you
You're an angel sent to me
I remember that when you looked in my eyes
I fell in love with your smile
[Bridge]
& I can say—you help my heart beat every day
& I believe I'll never be alone
You'll live in me . . .

Mandy Medicine

It felt like I was losing the people I cared about most. I felt alone and adrift.

And then came Mandy.

I'd known Mandy for a long time—she'd been dancing with me ever since I started performing as Hannah. One night in the middle of the tour we got out of the pool at some nasty hotel where the bus was parked. Mandy was going through a hard time with a friend of hers. I'd lost my first love. Vanessa was gone from this earth. Mandy and I sat on a bed in her hotel room and I said, "Hey, do you want to be best friends?" She said, "Yeah." It was out of the blue. Random. A joke. But then something amazing happened. Our BF promise took hold.

Mandy, how pumped are you that you get a chapter title?

7 people I can't live without

1. Mandy
2. my big sister
3. my mommy
4. Lesley
5. Ashley Tisdale
6. Auntie Edi
7. my mammie

Remember how I said that when you're on tour, away from home, people—friends, family—become your home? I'd been clinging a little too hard to my privacy. Vanessa's death reminded me to let myself need people. To stop pushing people away. To fight for friendship. Mandy and I act like kids together, like we're my little sister's age. A child's heart is so vulnerable, lighthearted, and fun. From the start we let our friendship stay young instead of being guarded and calloused. And it felt great. Like I was breathing again or that my heart was starting to heal.

After the tour finished, Mandy and I went on a big YouTube kick. We were hanging out, messing with the video camera while we worked up a dance routine, and just generally goofing around, and we decided to post it to YouTube. I swear doctors should write prescriptions for making YouTube videos. They're great medicine for a broken heart. At first it was just for fun, and then we were invited to do a "dance-off" with ACDC (the Adam/Chu Dance Crew), so we became M & M Cru and made some videos. That was cool, and it was still just for fun, but it was also lots of work with lots of people. So when that ended, we just went back to the basics, the old Miley and Mandy show, just us, goofing off—answering viewer questions like who our favorite bands are, interviewing my dad and sister. Or making a video of Mandy watching the scary maze game (an online prank), and Mandy freaking out. That might be my favorite.

My friendship with Mandy is more than videos and hanging out, of course. My little brother Braison is now way bigger than I am, and we had a huge fight, probably about something stupid like him giving me the wrong cell phone charger. Somehow it escalated to the point where he pushed me into the refrigerator and it actually hurt! I'm 5'4 and he's 5'10. Thirteen years old and 5'10—can you believe it? He's big. Anyway, I was pretty upset about the fight, and what I really want to say about Mandy is that I know if I need her, she'll be there. If I need a friend at four in the morning, she'll be there in five minutes, and she knows the same is true for me. Mandy is older than I am, so she helps me see a bigger picture. When I was upset about Braison, she came over and just stayed with me until I fell asleep. People might think it's weird, that it's too deep. But I think if you can't count on a friend for that, it's not a real friendship.

We're definitely going to have to make sure we line up boyfriends at the same time so we don't suffer withdrawal from each other.

Home Again

I know it sounds unbelievable, but shooting the first Hannah movie was relaxing. Yes, it was a full-length feature film. No, I'd never had a leading role in a movie before. Yes, I was in almost every scene. Yes, sometimes I had to act, sing, and dance simultaneously in coordination with up to 1500 extras. But I'd just spent four months living in a bus, performing for several hours, and sleeping in a different city every night. Then I'd gone straight to recording my album, *Breakout*. After all that, coming back to Tennessee—home!—where the movie was being shot—well, it was just about the most relaxing thing I could have imagined.

I slept every night at our farm in Franklin. My family was there. My animals were there. I could braid my horses' tails and watch the chickens live a little bit of their dumb, sweet lives every morning. Nights when I got to watch the sunset I just sat there and thought, *This is the biggest blessing*. Forget the movie. Forget the crazy work schedule and media madness that led up to the movie. Forget the demands on my time. Forget getting up and thinking "I need to wear this to look good." Forget the lack of privacy. When you're alone in the middle of 500 acres, it's all so far away. Nobody and nothing can get to you. It's a slower life. When Emily came to visit, she said, "I can see why you never wanted to leave your farm. It's so tranquil." And Emily's a city girl, through and through. Like I said: relaxing.

My favorite thing to do when I'm at home in Franklin is to go out on long horseback rides with my dad, the way we always have. Sometimes it seems like our horses are especially careful with me. They walk more slowly. They watch for holes. They've tripped before, but never with me. I've been riding them since I was so young, it's like they still think of me as a little girl who needs to be coddled. But during the movie, I was riding my horse Roam and he got startled by a snake in the grass. He spooked and started rearing and bucking.

Have you ever been in a car accident? You know how it seems to go so slowly? How you have time to think a hundred things in two seconds? That's how it was when Roam was bucking.

This may sound obvious, but never let a horse fall on top of you. Horses are big animals. I don't know, I figure some of our horses weigh a thousand pounds. I weigh around a tenth of that. Who's gonna win? Who's gonna hurt whom? It's easy to yell, "No, Roadie!" at a little two-pound dog. You know you're bigger and stronger. But when you're riding a horse, you have to stay in charge even though he's clearly the mightier beast. Even if you don't get hurt in a fall, if he steps on you by accident—you're a goner. My dad's had his foot broken by a horse. He said it feels like a car rolling over your foot.

All these thoughts flashed through my head as my horse jumped around and around. But I rode it out, rodeo style. (Wish the paparazzi had been there for that one!) I held on tight and stayed weirdly calm. I thought, *This horse will not drop me. We love each other.*

He's going to take care of me. He's going to protect me. He won't let me fall. Dad jumped off his horse and got me down as soon as Roam stopped kicking. Once my heart stopped racing, we headed back home. I didn't mention my little adventure on the set the next day. Needless to say, the movie people would not have been psyched if I'd nearly gotten trampled.

Oh, yeah—Emily's visit. For two seasons of *Hannah Montana*, Emily and I had struggled to get along. But we never hated each other. Now here we were, shooting our movie in Tennessee. On one of our days off, she had nothing to do, so she came over to hang out.

We went out on four-wheelers and drove out to a place on our property that we call the Shack. It's a falling-apart house that is older than time. There's antique junk everywhere—guns, medicine bottles, shoes. Emily and I crept up the rotting stairs, really carefully, holding hands. There had been a storm, and it seemed like the wind had blown up a whole new crop of treasures. There were bullets scattered across the floor. A column from an old newspaper. An icebox. (I guess the wind didn't stir *that* one up.)

Then we saw something fuzzy in the corner. Two fuzzy things, in fact. At first they looked like baby dinosaurs. It was so wild in the Shack, I thought maybe they actually *were* baby dinosaurs. Or a cross between a duck and a raccoon. Duckoons. Then I remembered that once there had been a hawk or a turkey—some huge bird—nesting in the chimney. These were baby birds! Baby birds that looked like duckoons. Emily and I just stood there and watched them for a long time. We didn't become blood sisters or swear best friends forever, but it was a great moment to share, away from the show and the movie and all the little squabbles we'd had. We rode home feeling the fresh air on our faces, and I could have sworn I felt something shift between us.

7 quirks I have

1. I always wear at least five bracelets.

2. I close one eye when I laugh.

3. I never wear blue and orange together (my middle school colors).

4. I hate the words <u>crusty</u>, <u>brothy</u>, and <u>creamy</u>.

5. I clean my room before I go to sleep every night.

6. my nickname is "one sock on" because one of my socks always falls off in my sleep.

7. I peel my nail polish off.

The Climb

When I read the script for the *Hannah Montana* movie, I was really happy. I didn't want it to be like an extra-long episode of the TV show. A movie should go further emotionally (and plotwise) than a half-hour comedy. The script had more depth than anyone expected, just what I was hoping for. I felt like I got to do much more serious acting.

During the TV series, I'd become more and more of a Method actor. In Method acting you use experiences from real life to summon emotions for your character. When you have to be sad, you think about things that upset you. I started talking about Hannah as if she were a real person, because I really thought of her that way. She existed in my mind. During the movie, when Hannah is kind of a brat, I acted a little like the bratty, fit-throwing Hannah when I went home. I mean, I didn't exactly throw fits, but I was quiet and grumpy and exploring the character in my head. And then, in the movie, when Miley was herself again and is eating Southern food and hanging out with her grandmother, I did the same thing.

7 ways I'm not like Hannah Montana

1. I'm not perfect
2. I don't like bright colors
3. I don't like heels
4. I don't wear a wig
5. I'm bad at secrets
6. I'm not cool
7. My dad's not really my manager (thank goodness!)

I worked nine hours a day dancing, singing, and acting, but being in Tennessee made the time fly by. I was home. My family was around, and Mammie was there with me all day long, every single day. The environment was familiar, even though I hadn't been to all the movie locations. For one scene, I sat in the middle of a vast field of daisies with big electric fans behind me blowing a soft wind through the flowers. If you didn't look at the cameras, the lights, or the fans, the setting was captivating.

The scariest moment came when I was shooting a scene with Lucas Till, who plays Travis Brody, my love interest in the movie. There's a scene where the two of us go to a waterfall where our characters used to hang out as kids. We were supposed to jump off a high rock ledge into the churning water of the water-fall. I'm a horrible swimmer. And I'd been eating crappy fried food for days. I was feeling fat and knew that my wet shirt would stick to all my bumps and lumps—not something I wanted on camera! But most of all I was scared of the big jump. And if that weren't enough, the water was cold. Ice cold. Dang it!

Fear is the only obstacle that gets in the way of doing what we love. People are scared to travel, to try new things, to follow their dreams. Fear holds us back from living the lives we were made to live.

Lucas had done his jump. Now he was treading water at the pounding base of the waterfall, waiting for me to plunge in. I stood at the edge of the ledge, but I just couldn't do it. It was so far down! I hadn't tested the water, but I knew how cold it was. I thought I was going to die. Poor Lucas was down there, shirtless, freezing, yelling, "Hurry! You've gotta jump!" Finally I went. It was really freaking cold. But, wow! The exhilaration was worth it. When I came out of the water the director said, "That was amazing, and your cankles look great!"

Right, about my cankles. They had become a big joke on the movie set. I'd tell the director, "I can't wear these shorts! They show my cankles," or I'd say, "I can't eat this fried dough—it's going straight to my cankles." And the director was always saying, "We need to try that again, but oh my gosh your cankles look fine." Or "Good job! I didn't even notice your cankles." I really meant it when I said I like to spin stuff in a positive way. "Cankles" may have bugged me at one point, but I took it and made it my own. Also, you have to admit it's just a funny word. So, there were my cankles, on full display for the movie cameras at the foot of a glorious waterfall in my hometown. Life could be worse.

Life *had* been worse. When we moved away from Nashville I was at a low point. The Anti-Miley Club— a few mean girls at school—was making me miserable. Of course I'd been back to Nashville loads of times since then, but now I was coming home as a full-fledged movie star. (Well, I wasn't exactly a movie star yet. I was still in the making-the-movie phase, but close enough.) When I performed with The Cheetah Girls, I felt like I was proving those mean girls wrong. Now I had nothing to prove. Those girls didn't matter at all anymore. They had no power to make me unhappy, and, through *Hannah Montana*, I was the one with the power. I had the power to make lots of people laugh. In my little piece of the world, it felt like a triumph of good over evil.

I'd left my Tennessee troubles behind, but it was still my home town. I didn't spend my childhood plunging into freezing waterfalls, but still, to have Miley Stewart come back to Tennessee, Miley Cyrus's home—it was life imitating art imitating life (like my dad always says). It tends to get me going in circles, thinking about how my character Miley's life is like mine and mine is like Miley's. *Hannah Montana* is all fiction, of course, but there's a thread through it that is connected with what's real in my world and the way I've been raised, being with my dad through the journey of music.

In the movie, I sing a song called "The Climb," which kind of captures the magic of what the show means to me. Dad always tells me that success is the progressive realization of worthy ideas or goals. That means that the best part—the part when you're most successful—is when you're taking steps forward toward your dream. When you're working to achieve it, not when you're on top. It's like Carl Perkins told me when he and my dad were rabbit hunting without guns. It's about enjoying the chase. **It's about having a dream and seeing it in the distance. It's about working for what you want. It's about the climb.**

At the end of the movie, as each actor finishes their part, they get "wrapped," which means the director announces that the person is done and the whole crew claps. On our last day of shooting, after everyone left had wrapped, they called out, "Mammie," who had sat there every day, no matter how hot it was or how long the shoot went. They wrapped Mammie, and everyone gave her a much-deserved standing ovation. It made me feel like my two families were now one.

Go, Mammie!

The Worst Trip
Ever

My album *Breakout* was released right after we finished shooting the movie. I immediately started doing publicity for the album and another movie, *Bolt*, an animated movie in which I am the voice of a girl named Penny.

When we were planning *Breakout*, I went into the studio with my producers, Antonina and Tim, and said I wanted to do an album that was more rock 'n' roll than pop. I wanted the album to be successful, duh, especially because it was my first Hannah-free album. But more than that I wanted it to be *my* music. The music I wanted to write.

At the 50th Grammy Awards, I presented an award

And yes, a lot of the songs were about breaking up with Prince charming! I'm human!

with Cyndi Lauper. We were hanging out backstage, talking about the Stones and other music—we seemed to have similar taste. And then she looked at me and said, "Well, don't be scared of anything. People waste their lives being scared. Lasso the moon. But don't do it because someone tells you it's the right idea." I got what she was saying. It was exactly what I was trying to do with *Breakout*. And I thought Cyndi Lauper was so cool that I added a cover of "Girls Just Wanna Have Fun" to the album.

Now it was time to promote it. In order to appear on *Good Morning America* I got on a plane in Los Angeles at seven p.m. It was me, my mom, and my sister Brandi on a private plane, and I don't know why, but Brandi and I just didn't sleep. We were too wired, playing Bon Jovi and Coldplay and watching the movie *Juno*. My mom kept telling me that I had to be on *Good Morning America* in just a few hours. In fact, it was already the same "morning." She reminded me that it was *live national television*. But eventually she gave up.

So we arrived in New York at three in the morning. I had to be at *Good Morning America* to get hair and makeup at 4:30. We checked into a hotel and tried to nap for half an hour. The three of us. In one bed. My mom is 5'7. Brandi is 5'6. I was curled up between them, trying to sleep, but Mom was all restless because she was so stressed about my being tired. It was a mess.

I "slept" for half an hour, went to hair and make-up, and showed up to do the sound check for the *Good Morning America* concert at six a.m. I performed at seven. The concert was no problem. The crowd gave me a rush, and I love performing. The concert finished at 8:30. Afterward, there was a half-hour meet and greet with a bunch of people. That's when I started feeling like a nap was in order. No such luck. I was due at the *Today* show.

In the car to the *Today* show, it hit me. Sleep. Must sleep. I dozed off and could have slept for hours. Unfortunately, it was only a seven-block car ride. Two minutes of rest is like eating one bite of a cookie— frustrating and completely unsatisfying. But there was no time for catnaps, much less naps. At nine o'clock I did a taped segment for *Today*. I tried my best, but I was so tired I don't even remember it. For all I know, I talked about how excited I was to be playing the role of Honky, Hannah Montana's prize-winning goose. Delirious. There were more interviews until eleven, when I spent an hour as the announcer at a marathon to promote *Bolt*. By then I could barely keep my eyes open. I did one more interview, then Brandi, my mom, and I got in the car to the airport. I watched out the back window as the paparazzi chased the car. I was home in L.A. by three p.m., and back at work the next morning. Surprise, surprise, I was sick as a dog.

That felt like the hardest day ever. I know promotion is important. I always try to be professional about it, even though it can be pretty grueling. But if I knew how exhausting it would be, then why didn't I sleep on the plane? That's the ten-million-dollar question, isn't it? Was it worth watching *Juno* with Brandi? Sure didn't feel like it the next morning. But this is the problem when you're sixteen and you have grown-up responsibilities. You don't stop being sixteen.*

* Until your 17th birthday!

I'm a kid. That's why, for the most part, we only did the big publicity and otherwise decided to let the album do whatever it was going to do. It was so weird not to do everything in my power to promote my first album under my own name. I am very proud of it and love what we came up with. But I also had to accept the reality of my situation. So much is happening all at once, so many opportunities. I want to make the most of them, but I also I need to stay sane.* There will be a day, my parents constantly remind me, when I won't have so much going on. And when that day comes, I don't want to feel like an empty shell of a person.

* Sleep, eat, have real friendships, spend time with my family.

Questions to Be Answered

Even though I didn't promote the album aggressively, I did and do give lots of interviews to TV, radio, and magazines. No matter how hard I try to keep it real, some of it is fake. Not fake because I'm lying or pretending to be someone I'm not, but fake because people ask me questions I can't answer. They ask, "What do you do with your free time?" How can I answer that? Stuff. I don't know. I want to say, "How do *you* spend *your* free time? On the computer? Yeah, me too." Or sometimes they'll ask, "What was your inspiration for '7 Things'?" **You already know the answer, everyone knows the answer, so why do you ask me?** They're trying to get me upset or make me uncomfortable, because that makes a "hot" interview. It's so hard to give a decent answer to "What's it like being Hannah Montana?" I've been asked that question at least ~~a hundred~~* times. Oh, and then there are all the supposedly smart media people who pretend to be completely confused by Hannah Montana, Miley Stewart, and Miley Cyrus. It's just not that hard. Watch one episode. You'll get it.

*make that a million

I always get asked: "What's it like working with your dad?" Nobody ever asks me about my mom, who is always always there for me. She's like a sister to me (and trust me, we fight like sisters), but she never stops being the mother who keeps me safe. You know, even if they did ask about Mom, I'd have trouble answering. I'll tell you this. She doesn't care about my job—she just wants me to be happy. And she's talented at what she does. She doesn't define herself by my success or try to live through me. She's a normal mom, a mom who loves me not because of what I do but because of who I am as a person. She's why I've been able to keep my head on straight.

Mom is so woven into my daily life I wouldn't know which strand to pull out to describe us. I mean,

I just called her because I have my big sweet-sixteen party this weekend, and I'm bloated and freaked out that my dress won't fit. Mom was absolutely calm, as always, saying, "Don't worry. We'll fix it." That's today, but can't you see how she's always there: replacing my dead fish, presenting me with a cheer-leading trophy, driving me from Toronto to Alabama for a bit part, getting me out of bed when my bad skin got me down, supporting me, grounding me, com-forting me, helping me find my way? She really is my hero, and I want to be just like her.*

As for my dad, it's so tough to answer what it's like being on a TV show with him. I always talk about how he is a best friend to me and how we put work away when we leave the set. I say the same answer over and over, a zillion times. And it's true. But—same as with my mom—how am I supposed to communicate every-thing that there is about my relationship with my dad in three sentences or less? It's impossible. I can never capture how we are together. Nobody can understand that. So I can't really answer the question genuinely. And it's not like they really want me to. They just want my little sound bite to fit neatly in

* OKay, this you can mention to Mom.

their magazine or TV show or radio spot. There's no way that space could contain a whole person. But I need them to promote my work. And they need me to promote their shows. So we all just keep on doing our jobs as well as we can. I try to be present, and I try to be real.

But about my dad . . .

More than Ovaltine

Well, here's my chance to talk a little bit about having such a great dad. I got really lucky. True, he couldn't be around all the time—he was often working in some other town for stretches of time. I never understood that when I was younger, but now I do, because I have to do the same thing. My little sister, Noah, will say, "Why do you have to leave?" And now I know that there's a show that has to go on. Whether it's *Hannah Montana*, a tour, or a recording session, there are other people involved. They're counting on me (and everyone else) to show up. I guess this is a lesson that lots of people learn when they start working. A job is a different responsibility from school. If you don't go to school, it's your loss.

But if you don't go to work, other people are affected, their families are affected. When my dad has to leave, he's just got to.

My dad has never had a nine-to-five job in my lifetime. We try to have breakfast every morning and dinner every night, but his schedule is pretty much always changing. That can be hard. But then, when he does come home, it's the best feeling in the world. For the next few weeks we have his complete attention, and we milk it for all it's worth.

What makes my dad so special is the time we spend together. How can I explain *time*? If we take a two-hour horse ride through the country around our house in Franklin, I can tell you where we went and what we did. I can describe the big, beautiful sky. I can tell you some of the words we exchanged, and how peaceful and exhilarating the silences were. I can even describe how my dad likes to lay some folk wisdom on me, telling me stories I've heard a million times, or how he likes to remind me that when he was at his professional peak, he didn't have anything, that being on this farm with his family is everything to him. Maybe that will help you understand. Our

Ovaltine mornings may be a sweet story, but even that probably doesn't do the trick. Maybe I should tell you that Dad wants "Over the Rainbow" played at his funeral because that's what Pappy wanted, but that I want us to dance to it at my wedding so we can give the song a new, happier association. But I'm not sure I believe in the power of words or music to truly capture what passes between two people. The best I can hope for is that you'll connect my description to something that is true for you.

The media has said some stuff about my dad and me being too close or too cuddly for a father and daughter. For me and my dad, it's not weird at all. And who cares if the public likes it or not? I think it's special that we're still a father and a daughter, that we love each other, that we aren't afraid to show it, and that we don't let other people tell us what expressions we're supposed to have on our faces when we take a picture together!

I say who cares, but of course it's hard not to care. I have feelings. It's painful to see some of those nasty comments on the Internet. I'm not saying everyone has to love me, but some people are so full of anger, hatred, and bitterness. When I'm not ignoring them or feeling hurt by what they say about me, I worry about the people who write those cruel comments. What made them so angry? Why are they sitting at home saying horrid things? Why aren't they at the mall with their friends?

When *Hannah Montana* got popular, I knew the media attention was going to come. True, I didn't expect the paparazzi to follow me around *all* the time, but I know it's part of the job. For the most part, I can let the gossip roll off my back. The first negative rumor about me was that I was pregnant. I was fourteen. I was just like, *Well, that's stupid.* I don't change my life. I try to treat the media—including the paparazzi—with respect. I treat them like friends. Heck, sometimes I see them more than I see my real friends. They're not going away. That's the way it is, and I live with it.

I try to be a good role model, and that's why I think it's too bad that lots of people hope to make money off my mistakes. I wish they could make money off my achievements. Actually, there are people who do that too. When I heard that a photo of me kissing someone (not a failure or an achievement—just a private moment) could earn someone $150,000, I told Brandi, "I'll send the picture to you, and then you can buy a house."

The only way I can respond to all of this is to put good into the world. Like Dad says (well, Newton, really), for every action there is an equal and opposite reaction. I'm aiming for the positive in whatever I do.

Duckoons

After the Best of Both Worlds tour, after we shot the *Hannah Montana* movie, after *Breakout* was released, after the worst trip ever, it was August, and I was craving a nice, long, well-deserved vacation. Preferably in the tropics. Ah, that *would* have been nice. But it was time for the third season of *Hannah Montana* to start shooting. I went straight back to work.

Over the summer when we shot the *Hannah Montana* movie, Emily and I got along fine. We were in a new place, and the work was different enough that whatever bad energy we had had seemed to be gone, or at least on hold. After the movie wrapped, we didn't talk until we came back to work. It's not that we weren't talking intentionally or out of spite. We just never had had that kind of friendship. But when we came back to work for the third season, something had changed. Yes, we did have fun together when she came to my farm in Franklin. And yes, we'd had another break. But there wasn't some big flash of lightning and suddenly things were great. It's not like those duckoons breathed a magic friendship spell on us or anything. When we came back, we just worked. We felt close. We weren't just getting along—we were great.

Now Emily and I love hanging out. We'll spend four days in a row together. I can't imagine a better Lilly. We're *super* close. Freakishly close for how much time we spend together. It took us a while to get into a groove—we both needed to learn how to be sensitive to each other. We never had a big blow-out fight followed by an old-fashioned heart-to-heart like I'm sure so many teenage friends do. Both of our lives are so busy that cycling through that kind of dramatic conflict and resolution is a luxury we can't afford. We work together every day. We're professionals. We wanted to get along, and we absolutely had to behave responsibly for the good of our show and our careers. So yeah, for a while I was just doing my best to keep the peace. But you know how they say that sometimes if you act a certain way long enough—act happy even when you are sad—eventually that happiness becomes real? Well, I think somewhere in the course of trying to keep the peace and act like friends, it sort of became true. It felt natural. And once it was natural, well, things were just peaceful. Getting along with Emily was a happy surprise. Work was a better place to be—it felt much more natural now that my onscreen BF suddenly felt like a real BF. It even feels weird now to try to talk about how tense and unpleasant it was. That was us? It's hard to believe.

Time passed, and now when I look at Emily I don't feel insecure or competitive or annoyed at our differences. Instead I see someone who has been with me through long, grueling work days and someone I can hang out with whenever there is a free moment.

It was worth it, worth all that fighting and tolerating. I figured out that your friends don't have to be exactly like you. In fact, the people who are different are the ones who are more likely to open the world for you. Those friendships can take the most work—I don't think I'd ever really worked on a friendship before this.* Maybe this is a lesson that everyone learns at some point in life. **The friendships that take work can be the ones that are the most rewarding.**

> *No, I don't think working on those sixth-grade girls would have helped in the least.

Now that I think about it, it's part of growing up, I guess, and part of having a grown-up job as a child. I see the days spinning by and look for ways to make my relationships strong, productive, happy, and peaceful. I'll always be hyper and impulsive, and I'll always talk without thinking, but I'm more aware of how my actions affect others, and what has to be accomplished, and what my responsibilities are. No matter how tired or goofy I feel, I have a greater sense of the big picture, and what I want to give and get from life, every day. I have Emily to thank for that lesson, because I have a feeling it's going to be something I come back to over the years.

The Bridge

Romantic relationships also take work. That I'm sure of. And they, too, change and grow.

The last time I saw Prince Charming, we hugged. I closed my eyes for a moment. It was a strange hug, but I did not want to let go. In that moment, I just wanted to imagine that it was two years ago, and things were the way they used to be.

When I write songs, I try to tell a whole story. But sometimes the whole story isn't ready to be told. The bridge of a song is the transitional part, the part that musically connects two parts of the song. It's sometimes called a climb. After the bridge, a song may come back to the chorus, but it's bigger, it's grander, and it feels different because of what happened in the bridge. When you hear the bridge, you feel things changing, and you know that the finale is near.

That's where I am these days. I'm in a different key. I'm still climbing, still figuring it out. I'm hurt and mad and happy and hopeful. Prince Charming was my first true love, and I'll hold a place in my heart for him forever.

So I'm in the bridge of a song. I know what the final chorus sounds like. I know it's coming. I expect it. I'm just not quite there yet.

You don't have to love me
for me to, baby, ever understand
Just know of the time
that we both had
And I don't ever
want to see you sad,
be happy
'Cause I don't want to hold you
If you don't want to tell
me you love me, babe
Just know I'm gonna
have to walk away
I'll be big enough for
both of us to say, be happy.
    —From "Bottom of the Ocean"

Sheba

When I was one or two, my mom gave my dad a dog named Sheba for Father's Day. It was a time in my dad's life when he was very successful—on top of the mountain—but he had the realization that he didn't have anything. So he let go of his music career and moved with the family and Sheba to the farm in Franklin to be the very best husband and dad he could be. Sheba was part of that, part of coming back home, part of choosing family over fame and fortune. Dad loved that dog—she was the most loyal dog ever. She was with us for a long time, but unfortunately Sheba didn't have a good end. She was bitten by a tick, got paralyzed, and then, because she couldn't move, she got hit by a car. My dad was devastated. That was a few years ago.

It was in June a couple of years ago that my parents were walking around Pasadena when they saw a beautiful black dog who reminded them of Sheba. She was with a homeless woman wearing a shirt that said ANGEL. Mom and Dad stopped to pet the dog and started talking to the woman, who said her name was Joanne. She said, "I'm a Christian. My husband and I got divorced. I feel like I'm supposed to be here on the streets. I'm a missionary." My dad asked what the dog's name was. Joanne said it was Sheba.

Sheba! My parents were touched by Joanne's story and the whole Sheba dog connection. They tried to give Joanne some money, but she wouldn't accept it. She said she was fulfilling her calling.

Now, I haven't talked much about religion and what God means to me and my family. I mean, you know I go to church on Sundays, but faith is more than that to me. It's part of who I am, the way I think, and how I live my life every day. Meeting Joanne— someone so dedicated to God—was important and meaningful to my parents. God has all kinds of messengers, and I always have my eyes, ears, and heart open.

Faith is having the strength to trust in something that you can't see with your eyes or prove scientifically. You believe because your heart tells you that's where you should go or who you should be. Your heart tells you what is right.

A few days later, it was the Fourth of July. We didn't have any plans. Remember? My parents aren't big planners or partyers. It was a hot afternoon, and we were all just walking around Pasadena. My dad mentioned Sheba and wondered if she was afraid of the fireworks the way our Sheba had been. We looked for Joanne but couldn't find her. Then my little sister—who'd never met Joanne—said, "Oh, look at that dog." She pointed across the street. It was Joanne and Sheba.

This time Joanne allowed my parents to give her twenty dollars. Dad wanted to take her in to the Cheesecake Factory to get something to eat. She was afraid to leave her cart, which made sense to me. It was her home, and it wasn't under lock and key the way most of us keep our treasured possessions. We guarded her cart for her while she went in. People looked at us funny, like we didn't belong, and I wondered if she got looks like that every day.

When Joanne reappeared, she was carrying Cokes for all of us. We talked with her for a long time that night. She said that these streets were her Africa, her Indonesia. Instead of going someplace far away, this was her mission field. Joanne was intelligent and calm. There wasn't a shred of bitterness in her. And she knew her Scripture. At the end of that night, my parents came right out and said, "Please let us help you get off the streets. You can come to our house. Or we'll get you a hotel and figure something out." Joanne smiled and said, "I hope you'll remember me, but you don't have to visit. Don't worry about me. I'm happy."

And it seemed to be true. Two months later my parents were back in Pasadena, and there she was, wearing a shirt saying I LOVE JESUS, and sitting with her dog. My parents couldn't fathom why someone would choose that life, but they had faith in her and the message she brought us. The person who we thought needed us the most didn't want anything from us. She was full of love. She was content. She didn't want or need anything from anyone. She lived in a park. She followed her calling. God took care of her. Like Mammie says, "All things work together for the good of those who love God" (Romans 8:28).

My mom grew up in a conservative church. For a long time she went to church because that's what you were supposed to do. Our whole family did. We were always looking for a good church to visit. Then, when I was in middle school, Brandi brought us to a new church in Franklin. The People's Church was different. It became a family for us. The members of our congregation hold each other accountable for the way we live our lives, and at the same time the church is a place where I have felt safe and unjudged, especially during those tough middle school years. For the first time, our family started making decisions based on our faith. I feel like we have more of a true relationship with God than we did when we went to church because it was a ritual. The People's Church really opened my heart. It has made me truly thankful.

A lot of people at our church wear purity rings, which represent a commitment to remaining celibate

Maybe she was an angel.

244

until you're married. When Brandi turned twenty-one, she asked my mom for a purity ring, and my mom bought one for her. Brandi has always been independent and good at knowing what she wants and believes. She's so honest to everyone, including herself. I love her and respect her and think she's beautiful inside and out. We always talked openly about her ring and what it meant. When Brandi's boyfriend (whom she plans to marry) comes to visit, he'll often stay for a week. Every night at eleven they go to their separate rooms. My parents aren't telling Brandi to do that. She does it because she respects herself that much.

When I got old enough and there were boys in the picture, I asked if it was time for me to get my own ring. My mom gave me one that has a circle on it, to represent the circle of marriage. There's a little diamond in the center of the circle for me, and when I get married, there will be another diamond added. But until then, it's just me. And it feels right.

The press might make fun of some people for wearing purity rings, but I don't pay attention to that. They can think what they want. I have my morals!

I also bring my faith to my career choices. I

already told you that our family talks about being light in a dark world—when it comes to my work I try to do projects that I can be proud of. I love that *Hannah Montana* is a sweet, good quality show that brings joy to people's lives. As I start doing more grown-up, dramatic projects, I want to stick with what I believe and what makes sense for a girl my age. I want to be a good role model. That's why I signed on to work with the writer Nicholas Sparks. His books and movies show strong morals, and loving, hard relationships. I can do meaningful work—without compromising my values.

The Happiest Place
on Earth

As I've said, a big part of my faith is helping others, not out of guilt or gratitude for what I have but because it feels right and necessary. It's true that my sweet sixteen was a huge, over-the-top affair. We shut down Disneyland on a school night; five thousand people attended the party, and each one paid $250 for the privilege. Hey, girls who bullied me in sixth grade, check this out: thousands of people paid cash dollars to come to my birthday party! But it was nothing like those sweet sixteen extravaganzas you see on MTV.

Before you think I'm a selfish nutjob for charging people to come to my party—here's the reason: the event raised one million dollars for Youth Service America. *All* that money went to a good cause. Like I've said, if I'm gonna be in the spotlight, I want to use my powers for good.

The evening of the birthday party was pretty choreographed—I knew what was supposed to happen and when it was supposed to happen. But the biggest moment was something that none of us planned or expected. My good friend Lesley, whom I cheered with for all those years, flew in from Tennessee to come to the party. She was staying with me at my house, and right before we headed to Disneyland I said to her, "I'm so happy. The only thing that would make me happier would be for Pappy to be here for the party." Lesley told me not to be sad. She said, "He's here. He's watching."

Near the beginning of the celebration, at a little reception for the celebrities who were attending, my mom was supposed to give me my birthday present. But as it happened, the party was running late. By the time my mom gave me my present, the celebrities were already in cars for the parade. So the only people left were my mom, Rich Ross and Adam

Sanderson (execs at Disney), and Aunt Edi, my mom's best friend. It was just a small group of people who felt like family.

Then my mom surprised me with a Maltipoo, a tiny all-white puppy who is part Maltese, part poodle. A puppy! I was so excited. Okay, it wasn't a total surprise. My mom knew I was dying for a puppy, and I had a feeling that wish might come true.

Animals are mysterious, interesting, amazing creatures. You can't ever know exactly what they're thinking, but you know how they feel because of the way they treat you. Their emotions are honest and pure. A dog whines when she's tired. She whines when she's hungry. She snuggles when she's happy. She licks your face when she's happy to see you. She jumps up and down and bites your shoes when you get home. Animals treat you the way friends should. I mean, I don't want my friends to lick my face. But when friends want to show you how much they care and are excited to see you, they sometimes get embarrassed or feel silly. Animals don't think they're better or worse than you are. They don't get embarrassed. They just love you.

So we were playing with the puppy and taking pictures, and then my mom said, "Sofie, look at the camera Sofie." I froze in disbelief. Time stood still for a second. Then I blurted out, "Sofie—that's Pappy's dog!" My mom hadn't realized—Sofie the puppy had come from the breeder with her name— but Sofie the dog had been Pappy's dearest friend, his trusty companion. She was everything to him. I had no doubt in my mind that this fluffy little puppy wriggling in my arms was my birthday present from Pappy. God had sent me a gift from my pappy. When I had that realization, I started crying. I sat there in front of everyone, just weeping, with Sofie in my lap reaching up to lick my tears away.

I'm glad all the celebrities were already shuttling off to the parade. It was such a sweet, special, over-whelming moment that I'm happy I was surrounded by people who know me well. Plus Pluto. Pluto the dog was there too. (Another moment of deep respect for those who can wear heavy costumes with small air holes.) I guess that guy in the Pluto suit is kinda part of the family now. He (or she?) probably thinks I'm a pretty emotional girl. But the truth is, in all the other big moments in my life so far, I usually haven't cried or gotten superemotional. On that night, though, I kept saying, "Oh my gosh," and my eyes would well up again. I just could not stop crying. I will remember that moment for the rest of my life.

Right after that was the parade. We started driving down the street, through crowds of kids lining the streets of Disneyland. As if I didn't have reason enough to be emotional, our car rolled slowly down the street past people yelling my name, screaming Happy Birthday. I didn't know how to react. I felt kind of embarrassed and stupid, and at the same time I felt like a princess. I was wearing a gorgeous champagne gown beaded with crystal, and pretty aqua blue pumps covered in Swarovski crystal beads. They were real Cinderella shoes. But still . . . I sank down in my seat. My mom nudged me and said, "Honey, wave like a beauty queen." I said, "But I feel dumb! It's so weird that all these people are here to see me."

Embarrassment wasn't the only emotion I was feeling. Yes, I've done concerts in front of thousands of people, but this felt different. It felt so personal, so intimate. I really couldn't believe so many families were there to support me and celebrate with me. There were reporters in the car with me, trying to interview me, and I could barely answer. I'd start talking, then get choked up, then start laughing at myself. I was laughing and crying the whole ride.

The best kind of laughter is when you start laughing for no reason and can't stop. In that moment, you forget about everything else. You let go of the world, and let go of control—which we all should do sometimes.

Then we got to the purple carpet. That's right, purple! I love purple. Remember when I walked down my first red carpet, at the premiere for *Chicken Little*, and nobody had any idea who I was? Now the carpet was custom-colored for me! Wow.

Sometimes this life I'm leading starts to feel normal. Walking down red carpets starts to feel like an everyday thing. Even if you love it—which I do—the excitement gets consumed by the fact that it's work. But that night, the unbelievable reality of my life rushed at me. I felt so blessed.

Even though I've walked on red carpets before, this time was different, and not just because of the color of the carpet. Everyone there was a friend of mine: Emily, Mitchel, and Moises Arias (who plays Rico). Anna Maria Perez de Tagle and Shanica Knowles (who play Ashley and Amber) both told me they were wearing purple dresses for me. Demi Lovato was there—there were so many Disney people it felt like a family reunion. I did interviews and talked to friends and fans in between. That part was really relaxed and fun.

Then it was time for me to perform. Which meant a new outfit, of course. My wardrobe designer, Dahlia, surprised me with a vest that said "Sweet Sixteen" on the back. Cool! I know it might seem strange that I performed at my own party, but I figured people paid $250 a ticket! I wanted to give back to them.

The show started on Tom Sawyer Island. Dad opened for me. He played "Ready, Set, Don't Go" and there was a montage of photos and videos of my life up till now. It was so sweet. It doesn't matter how many times I hear my dad sing that song. I know why he wrote it and I know that it's real for us every time.

After Dad, I sang, and then—this was the best part of all—Disney presented the million-dollar check to Youth Service America (YSA), and we honored ten of YSA's "Service Stars," just a few of the amazing kids who don't let being young stop them from working hard to make this world a better place. I was so into it—I was jumping up and down like a little girl.

Next my dancers and I got on a boat. I sang two more songs as they took us out onto the river. The boats went right up into the crowd. It was really cool way to perform, floating right up to the crowd and seeing the sparkling lights of Disneyland all around us.

Gosh, it all happened so fast that I was like, Oh, right, the boat!

I had a break after the concert to cool down and clean up. I changed into a beautiful baby blue dress with sequins and baby blue feathers around the bottom. Finally, it was time for the big birthday moment. I've had birthday parties before. I've blown out candles and had people sing "Happy Birthday" to me. But I never imagined I'd be standing in front of Cinderella's castle, gazing at a gigantic cake that won a "Design a Cake for Miley's Birthday" contest, surrounded by sixteen foot-tall candles, while thousands of people sang for me. I "blew out" the candles (they were electric—it must have been someone's job to make sure they turned off at the exact right moment), and the instant the candles went out, the fireworks started. Fireworks!

How did I feel at that moment? I can't really say. It was too big to absorb, and I still haven't really taken it in. I just know that it was a night I never could have imagined. An amazing, unforgettable night. But it also had a bigger purpose. It raised money for a great cause, and that's what makes it much more meaningful than the celebration of one sixteen-year-old's birthday.

After the party was over and all the friends left our suite, it was midnight. The park was empty and closed, and I was allowed to ride the rides. Can you imagine? Disneyland, all to myself. It was a once in a lifetime opportunity. But I was sooooo tired. We rode two rides, and then I turned to Mom and said, "Let's just go home." And so we did.

A New Kind
of Tour

*Sorry! I get a little bit off topic sometimes!

Like I've said,* life has been a roller-coaster ride from the moment I got on *Hannah Montana*. When the whole book was happening, I was in the middle of filming the *Hannah Montana* movie, working on songs for the soundtrack, and doing all the other stuff that makes up my day. I was SWAMPED!**

**Don't get me wrong—busy is good! I love being busy. Even when I have downtime, I fill it up. The other night I was up till 4 in the morning... cleaning my room! Just because I couldn't NOT be busy!

But I was—and am—so proud of the book that I was eager to get on the road to talk about it when it was finished. There were so many stories I wanted to share! Now, I've been on my music tours, and I've done promotion for my CDs and for *Hannah Montana*, but a book tour was different. I was going to be meeting people who had gotten a glimpse into some pretty personal parts of my life. I was going to hear what they had to say—good and bad. And this was the scary part—I was going to have to talk about all of this stuff out loud, on TV and on the radio.

My mom knew I was a little stressed. So, like she always does, she made me feel better. She told me to remember that I share things all the time with my fans through my songs.

It's funny: even though I'm goofy and like to do silly things like make videos and post random thoughts on Twitter*—I'm actually pretty private... *used to! especially about writing. When I first come up with an idea for a song, I like to be alone. Writing songs has always come so naturally to me. The idea gets in my head and flickers around. A chord pops up that goes with it. A few beats bounce together and then—a song. But it always starts when I'm by myself. When I'm sitting on a porch or up in my room or even out on the tour bus.

Writing a book was almost the same process.* I *Minus the beats and was at no loss for things to talk about. Like I've said, chords! I like to talk. But from the start, I was forced out of my safe and private space. I couldn't do it all on my own. I had to ask my family questions, dig into our history. There was fun stuff—hearing my dad talk about what I was like when I was a kid. And there was sad stuff—like remembering my last conversation with Pappy. But while it wasn't all rainbows, I had to keep reminding myself—a chapter is almost like a song. Once I could think of the book that way, it was easier to tie things together. I'd get an idea, like I do when writing songs, for a chapter, and let it bounce. Eventually, I'd make it something bigger. But I liked starting small. Sort of the story of my life!

I'm not saying I did it perfectly! But I tried!

Back to the tour. At the same time that the book was coming out, we were debuting the first single off of the *Hannah Montana* sound track. I may have mentioned it before—"The Climb."* Now, as you all know because I've talked about it a lot, that song means a LOT to me. So to be out talking about that AND the book was a pretty awesome experience.

*Sound familiar?

Even though I had been pretty nervous about talking about the book, it was fun to hear people responding to it. **Each person took away something different, which is exactly what I like about writing. Whether it is a love song, or a sad poem, or a book about your life so far, everyone sees it a little differently.** Through one person's eyes, the bullies in my life might not have meant anything, but the move from Tennessee to California might have been devastating. It is, like the saying goes, all in the eye of the beholder.

Paging Miley Cyrus

We made three stops for the book—New York City, Los Angeles, and then home to Nashville. I honestly didn't know what to expect. Like I said, I've done other types of tours—but would this be the same? Would the fans wait in line to buy a book? Apparently, yes. When I got to the New York store, the line was out the door and around the block. It was crazy!

At one point, before they let people in, I peeked out the window that looked down on the street. There were fans lined up for blocks, and each one was holding my book. Some were reading and smiling. Others were leafing through the pictures. But ALL of them were excited about a book that I wrote. It was kind of one of those great moments when you realize that there is a lot of good you can do in this world. I'm not saying that my book is going to single-handedly stop illiteracy, but if I got one of my fans to read who wouldn't have before, that's pretty fantastic. Those are the moments I really thank God for *Hannah Montana*.

7 things I love about books

1. they can make me smile
2. they can make me cry
3. if I want to pretend I'm some-one else, they are a great solution
4. most of the time, they have happy endings
5. they can create a fake reality
6. they can teach me things I never knew
7. they can capture moments pictures can't

Doing the signing in New York and another one in L.A. had been pretty great. But coming home to do one in Nashville was the icing on the cake. It felt like coming full circle, the same way it had felt to film the movie in Tennessee. This was my chance to share with my town all the reasons I loved it. To really show people how growing up in Nashville had helped make me the person I am today. How the city is always in my heart and always keeping me grounded—no matter where I am. I had written it all down. Everyone could know now, and I was so excited.

The store in Nashville was smaller than the other two had been, but I'm pretty sure the crowd was bigger. And rowdier.* People showed up that I never thought I'd see again. One of my old teachers was there. A girl who had gone to my school told me she had been bullied too. Another group of kids showed up from one of the organizations I volunteer for. Their joy and love were overwhelming.

Before I knew it, the signing was over.

Remember how I said I like to stay busy? Well, that day was a perfect example. Not only was I doing the signing, I was going to make a surprise appearance at a Nashville movie theater for a screening of *Hannah*

*No surprise! Yee-haw, Nashville!

Montana: The Movie. That meant a whole new round of butterflies in my stomach! What if the audience hated it? So you know what I did? I ordered up some good ole Southern comfort food—chicken and dumplings—and sat down for a meal. I'm sure I was a sight! All around me people were getting ready—dresses got brought in, my makeup team arrived, and I just sat in the middle, chowing down. I admit, stuffing your face full of food right before you are supposed to stuff *yourself* into a fancy dress might not be the best idea, but hey, those dumplings did the trick. I was energized and ready, and by the time I stepped onto the red carpet...the butterflies? They were long gone.

No one gets in the way of my chicken and dumplings!

♡
Hopefully Not the Last Song

You know how I've said I don't know what I want to do in the future?* Well, I know that movies are definitely a part of it. Filming the *Hannah Montana* movie had been such an amazing experience. Being with my fellow cast members through those months and then getting to see all that work pay off when the movie premiered? That was fantastic. There was so much of Miley Cyrus in Miley Stewart and Hannah Montana that if it had tanked, I would have kind of felt the audience didn't like me. But they did! So all that hard work—the hours of repeating the same scene over and over again—was worth it.

But filming *The Last Song* was a whole new experience. I was working with a new character—

*I have a list of 7 things I want to be when I grow up because I can't narrow it down!

Seriously y'all. I think I can do the Hoedown Throwdown in my sleep.

264

someone totally different from Hannah or Miley Stewart. All the lessons I had learned filming the TV show were going to have to come into play again— getting into character, finding the voice I wanted, feeling the emotion. But whereas I have had years to do that with Hannah, I was only going to get months to work on *The Last Song*.

This was a Nicholas Sparks movie. AND he had written it with me in mind.* I wanted to make sure that this was the best performance of my life so far. Luckily, I had a pretty great group of people to work with...and Tybee Island. Have I mentioned that place before?** From the moment I walked onto the set, I felt like I was Ronnie Miller. She is a tough girl struggling to find her place in the world, and I grabbed on to that. And the best part was that everyone involved grabbed on to their parts. We became this tight little family there on Tybee Island. My co-star, Liam Hemsworth, and I would film a scene on the beach and then, as soon as the director called Cut, I'd be jumping in the water, splashing around. Like I said, Tybee is a magical place. I think being there, we all felt like we were getting this break from reality.

I was so incredibly sad when filming ended.

*No pressure!

**Kidding! You know I love it there!

I hated saying good-bye to my new family. But I have such amazing memories from my time there. I wrote some fantastic songs and had some unbelievable moments.

Like when, after a long day of shooting, we all headed into the tiny town to grab food. And of course, the magic and emotions were getting to me. We sat down to eat and then noticed a band was playing. I sat there for a while, just enjoying the music and feeling like for once, the world had stopped spinning so fast. And then someone called out my name and before I knew it, I was up there, singing along! In this restaurant on an island off the coast of Georgia! How random? But it was moments like that that made *The Last Song* such fun. You never knew what the day would bring. Sometimes horrible storms would come in, and we'd have to stop filming. Other days it was so sunny and beautiful, all you wanted to do was sit on the beach. **But I guess that is sort of what life is—a series of storms to weather before the clouds clear and the skies turn blue. And if you can learn to appreciate them both, you're in for a pretty sweet view.**

Living the Dream

I don't act or sing for awards. I don't do it for the money. Those things are nice benefits of my work, but they don't drive me.

I do it all for the passion of the art. I love making music, performing, and bringing something special to the people who listen and watch. Stevie Wonder is blind, and it doesn't matter if his awards shine like diamonds or are dull, dark rocks, so long as he loves his music. Beethoven still made music after he lost his hearing. When you take your senses away and still love what you're doing, that's when you know it's your calling.

⋇　　⋇　　⋇

Hebrews 13:5-6

DON'T LOVE MONEY; BE SATISFIED WITH WHAT YOU HAVE. FOR GOD HAS SAID, "I WILL NEVER FAIL YOU. I WILL NEVER ABANDON YOU."

Although I know I'm earning a lot of money, it goes into some mysterious account somewhere and doesn't really affect me. I'm just doing the work that makes me happy. Pappy always said, "Love what you do for a living and you won't have to work another day in your life."

I don't have a big fat wallet or credit cards to buy whatever I want. It's one benefit of being a child star: that later on, when I do have access to the money, I'll be able to look back at this time and know that I was happy following my dream without material rewards. I hope I won't need that lesson, but I'm glad it's there for me. **At the end of life, all you have is what you felt as you were going through life.** Pappy said this, and now that Pappy's gone Dad says it, too. You don't have cool bags and a list of parties you were invited to. Press clippings, even music albums: none of the achievements or material things matters in the end. You can't take them with you. What really matters, and what you have in your heart at the end of your days, is the love and joy you lived and gave.

People sometimes ask me if I feel like I'm missing out on having a normal childhood. Do I ever think about the what-ifs? Would I do anything differently if I could do it all over again?

After all I've seen (the hardest childhoods) and all I've experienced (living my dream) it would never occur to me to dwell on what I might be missing. I know that I'm not going to a real school. I'm not attending homecoming games or a prom. I can't go to a movie without being recognized and all that entails.

Yes, there are fun parts of being a normal teenager that I haven't experienced and never will. And sure, there are a lot of days when I don't want to wake up at 6:30 every morning.* There are days when I don't get enough sleep and don't want to get up at all. Sometimes the set feels like a prison. There are certain sacrifices I am making. And there are sacrifices my family is making for me. In the quieter moments, which are few and far between, I think about what I'm missing. I wonder, but

m sure
e same
ning
ould
happen if
I went to
school

I don't wish. It's all worth it when I watch an episode of *Hannah* on TV, or see my new movie, or play my new CD for a child in the hospital. The good outweighs the bad. It isn't right to complain. I don't. I can't. I can't imagine holding on to the negative when there is so much that is great in my life.

I found my dream early. I'm living it. Lots of people find their dreams. I think the only way I'm different is that my dream just happened to come true before I entered high school. I feel grateful. I know how fortunate I am. I'm not so naïve that I think any dream is achievable for any person in any country on this earth. **But I do know this for certain—that you'll never find your dream if you don't reach for it as far and as high as you can.**

DREAM
with Brandi

Follow your dreams
Follow your heart
Show everyone in a gloomy sky
You can be a shining star
Don't lose your faith
'Cause there might come a day
When everything could disappear
Oh, but your dreams will still be here.

Things Happen for a Reason

When my mom was pregnant with me, my dad called her from the road. He says he had a vision. An instinct. The same way Dad plays music by ear, he likes to play life by ear. He says his intuition told him that the baby in my mom's womb was destined to be something that represented the light. Something positive. He said, "You know what? I just feel like that little baby is Destiny Hope Cyrus." When Dad's famous intuition talks, we listen. So Mom said, "That's it. That's her name." But as soon as I was born I became "Smiley," then "Smiley Miley," then Miley. I don't think anyone ever actually called me Destiny, so I decided to legally change my name to Miley.

My parents named me Destiny Hope because they believed that my destiny was to bring hope to people. My life does feel driven by destiny right now, but maybe that's only because my biggest dreams are actually coming true. Most people go through ups and downs, successes and failures, to figure out their true calling. My dad was a boxer for a long time, and then he thought he'd be a baseball player. But then he had a dream that told him to buy a left-handed guitar and start a band. He did, and the rest is history. I came across my calling early, and there is always the chance I could fail.

While I was growing up, my dad would remind me that Thomas Edison failed 10,000 times when trying to make a storage battery. When a reporter asked Edison about his failures, he said, "I have not failed seven hundred times. I have not failed once. I have succeeded in proving that those seven hundred ways will not work." I get it. **The most important ingredient in success is failure.**

Mandy sometimes calls me the most unlucky lucky person in the world. My heels break. My hair dryers blow. I got stuck on the Revenge of the

Mummy ride at Universal Studios. I was stuck in Splash Mountain at Disneyland for half an hour. I was standing on the red carpet with Taylor Swift and Katy Perry, and a bee came up and stung one of us. Which one? Me, of course (unlucky). A few days ago, I was at the mall with Mandy and I had my period and no tampons (unlucky). I went to the bathroom to buy one, but I had no change (unlucky). Then something changed. As I stood that day staring at the tampon dispenser, four tampons fell out of it, right into my hands (lucky!). And later when I withdrew twenty dollars from an ATM, the machine gave me sixty bucks (lucky!).* The way I think of it is that the little bad moments make the little good moments better. That doesn't mean I necessarily enjoy forgetting my lines or messing up a dance move, but weathering all those everyday frustrations and victories helps us practice for the bigger disappointments that are sure to come along.

I don't know how long my fame and success will last, but if years from now I'm playing coffeehouses instead of stadiums, that's okay so long as I'm still inspired and still inspiring a few people. I'll keep

* I returned it, of course!

doing my art. And, like I said when I talked about my sixteenth birthday party: for now, while the spotlight is on me, I want to use it well. I have an opportunity to make a difference in the world. I may have changed my name, but that doesn't mean I'm saying no to the destiny my parents envisioned for me. I don't want Hope as a middle name. But I sure want to try to bring it to everyone I meet or touch. I wrote a song called "Wake Up America" about taking care of our planet. It's on my album *Breakout*, which to date has sold over a million copies. How many chances do we have to remind that number of kids that this is their planet to love and save? That we have to protect the future? I have that chance, and I want to make the most of it. I meet kids in hospitals and schools and hope I can make them smile for that one quick moment, and I want to keep doing bigger things for organizations like City of Hope and Youth Service America that really make a long-term difference.

How could I be born into a name like Destiny Hope and not believe that things happen for a reason? Life is unpredictable. Nothing is written in stone. I've told you about myself, but I can't really say who I'll be. There's no right or wrong, success or failure. I don't look at things as black or white. My life won't be a series of either/ors—musician or actor, rock or country, straitlaced or rebellious, this or that, yes or no. The real choices in life aren't that simple. I think of it more like a story that keeps moving forward, with plain old days and then surprises that turn everything upside down. I don't set limits for myself. I want to be the best I can be. I want to dream big, but dreams change.

What I want, who I want to be, how I want to spend my time—keeping these questions open is good. It's life. I'm living every day of my life. When you think like that—and when you're only sixteen—then you're living a story that has chapter after chapter of blank pages ahead. **If there's one message I have for my fans, it's that you can make your dreams real, but you have to enjoy just being. Make the best of the life you have every day. I can't wait to see what's in the days ahead, but I also don't want to fill them up too fast.**

7 things I might be when I grow up

1. photographer
2. musical director
3. music teacher
4. writer
5. composer for movies
6. pilot
7. dog walker

Afterword:
Before I Sleep

When my dad tells me that for every action there's an equal and opposite reaction, he doesn't usually stop there. He reminds me that life is a series of ups and downs, peaks and valleys for everyone in every walk of life: farmers, businessmen and women, people who work in steel mills like Pappy did. And it's a whole lot harder to come down than it is to go up. But in the valleys, you find out who you really are.

My parents both talk about the day when all this slows down. My mom thinks I'll enjoy life more. My dad thinks I'll have more time to take it all in. But I know I'm blessed for this moment. I love my work. If

I don't work this hard forever, I don't know what I'll do with all the extra time and energy, though I have a few ideas (see the next few pages). I may have to get really, really good at calligraphy.

Even with a party to look forward to, I didn't want my sixteenth birthday to come. I love being the baby and thought that might stop. I don't even have any idea how to do my own laundry. (That's one of the ways in which my mom has babied me a little.) I have plenty of grown-up responsibilities—working full-time while still doing schoolwork, having meetings, meeting deadlines. My mom knows I need to be a kid sometimes, to feel safe and cared for and be driven around—though I hope that last one ends the second I get my license.

But yeah, I'm going to have to figure out the laundry thing at some point before I leave home. And you know what? I'm kind of excited. Because no matter what I do, even if its just a load of laundry, I'll be traveling forward, making my own future—and there are still miles and miles to go.

After the After

In the original afterword, I wrote that I was scared to grow up. But I think I might have already done it—without even knowing. I mean, not totally. Like I said, I do still have miles to go. But the experiences of the past year have pushed me forward in ways I'd never have imagined. I sat on a beach and came to grips with letting go. I opened my heart and fell in love again. I lost love but gained friendship. I traveled to new countries and went back home to familiar places. And, you'd be proud to know, I learned to do my laundry!

At least I have my own car now!

Still, those are only a few lessons. Only a few of the mile markers. There are more to come. Some of them I can guess, some of them are going to be surprises. And you know what? I can't wait.

100
things I want to do
before I die

1. ~~ride in a helicopter~~ DONE
2. go to the bottom of the ocean
3. get married/have kidz
4. stand on the Great Wall
5. go skydiving
6. ride in a hot air balloon
7. backpack through Europe
8. win a Grammy
9. personally help feed another country
10. meet Isaac Pablo
11. open summer camp for kids with H.L. or D.S.
12. draw awareness to teen pregnancies
13. go on a peace mission in Africa
14. swim in the Red Sea

15. pay Mammie's bills
16. learn to surf
17. ~~write my life story~~ DONE, I GUESS? (for now!)
18. have a wig co. for kidz
19. go to Hawaii for my b-day
20. build a school
21. rent a cottage in Surrey
22. design leather/wool-free uggs
23. read the entire Bible—**in process**
24. see the northern lights
25. shop in Milan
26. go to Egypt and see Tut's tomb
27. go to Jerusalem
28. run a marathon
29. fly a plane
30. get a motorcycle license
31. cross the country
32. live in TX
33. climb Mt. Everest
34. live out of the country
35. be 2 places @ once
36. visit kids in a hospital in all 50 states

37. ride a horse on the beach!
38. get my sister a Husky puppy
39. make a country album
40. do a metal record
41. introduce this generation to
    Buddy Holly and have him be on
    top ten albums on iTunes
42. buy my pappy's house.
43. go fishing and actually catch a fish
44. go to Fiji
45. produce my little sister's record
46. build my parents a house on
    the beach in Seaside
47. live with a family in Thailand
    and experience their day
48. dig a well in Indonesia
49. invent something . . . I don't
    know what yet, ha-ha!
50. finish this list and get to 100!!!!